Macrobiotic Cooking

is a culinary method with a whole philosophy behind it, representing hundreds of years of Eastern and Western thought. The macrobiotic principles applied to foods result in a remarkably varied diet that is very inexpensive, delicious to eat, easy to prepare—and in harmony with the natural chemistry of our bodies.

This book is an introduction to macrobiotic cooking as part of the macrobiotic way of life—the first step toward the attainment of spiritual health, emotional happiness, and physical well being through "oneness" with the universe.

Everything you need to know, from where and what to buy to how and when to cook it, is included—along with dozens of sumptuous recipes. For those who've tried macrobiotic cooking before, this is an important book; for those who haven't, it is essential.

Other SIGNET Titles of Related Interest

☐ **PLEASE STOP KILLING ME! by Ernest E. Snyder.** An alarming and frightening view of the modern world and the serious problems created by the science and technology that simultaneously produce our high standard of living and may well terminate us. (#Y4584—$1.25)

☐ **LET'S EAT RIGHT TO KEEP FIT by Adelle Davis.** Sensible, practical advice from America's foremost nutrition authority as to what vitamins, minerals and food balances you require, and the warning signs of diet deficiencies.
(#W4630—$1.50)

☐ **THE ROOTS OF HEALTH by Leon Petulengro.** The passport to good health is in the natural food that grows all around in the fields, hedges and gardens. The author tells you how to keep healthy by using the right foods, truly the "roots of health." (#T4267—75¢)

☐ **ROCKWELL'S COMPLETE GUIDE TO SUCCESSFUL GARDENING by F. F. Rockwell and Esther C. Grayson.** Everything you need to know from planning your home grounds to planting and maintaining them, including a handy calendar guide and a region guide based on the growing season, from the winners of the Citation for Horticultural Achievement of the American Horticultural Society.
(#Y4132—$1.25)

THE NEW AMERICAN LIBRARY, INC., P.O. Box 999, Bergenfield, New Jersey 07621

Please send me the SIGNET BOOKS I have checked above. I am enclosing $_____(check or money order—no currency or C.O.D.'s). Please include the list price plus 15¢ a copy to cover handling and mailing costs. (Prices and numbers are subject to change without notice.)

Name_____

Address_____

City_____State_____Zip Code_____

Allow at least 3 weeks for delivery

Macrobiotic Cooking

by Eunice Farmilant

A SIGNET BOOK from
NEW AMERICAN LIBRARY
TIMES MIRROR

Copyright © 1972 by Eunice Farmilant

All rights reserved

SIGNET TRADEMARK REG. U.S. PAT. OFF. AND FOREIGN COUNTRIES
REGISTERED TRADEMARK—MARCA REGISTRADA
HECHO EN CHICAGO, U.S.A.

SIGNET, SIGNET CLASSICS, SIGNETTE, MENTOR and PLUME BOOKS
are published by The New American Library, Inc.,
1301 Avenue of the Americas, New York, New York 10019

First Printing, May, 1972

PRINTED IN THE UNITED STATES OF AMERICA

This book is dedicated with love to my family and to all those who have chosen to open the doors of discovery through macrobiotics.

FROM FOOD, *verily, are produced all creatures—whatsoever dwells on earth. By food alone, furthermore, do they live, and to food, in the end, do they return, for food alone is the eldest of all beings, and therefore it is called the panacea for all.*

—UPANISHAD

Contents

Foreword	xiii
Introduction	xv
How I Got into Macrobiotics	19
The Meaning of Macrobiotics	21
Yin and Yang	22
Eating Whole Foods	26
Why We Cook Our Foods	27
Stocking Your Kitchen	32
Storing of Food	37
Utensils Are Your Basic Tools	40
Vitamins, Minerals, Proteins, etc.	45
Just Because It's Edible...	54
Grains	60
BROWN RICE	61
BARLEY	68
KASHA	70

x Contents

CORN	72
OATS	74
MILLET	75
WHEAT	77
WHEAT PRODUCTS	79
CRACKED CEREALS	80
FLAKES OF GRAIN	81
GRAIN MILK	82
SPROUTS	82
NOODLES	83
Breads and Other Things from Flour	86
UNYEASTED BREADS	88
RICE KAYU	89
CHAPATIS	91
PANCAKES, CREPES AND WAFFLES	92
PIE CRUST DOUGHS	
The Vegetables—Our Secondary Foods	95
Tempura	109
Salads	114
The Sea Vegetables	119
Pickles	124
Soups	127
Beans	137
Miso	142
Tofu	145
Special Dishes	147
Sauces	158
Desserts	165
Beverages	176
Putting It All Together	181

The Foods from Yin to Yang	187
But How Can I Travel and Still Eat This Way?	189
Stores and Restaurants in the U. S.	191
Stores, Restaurants, and Centers Outside the U.S.	204
Wholesale Distributors in the U. S.	208
Macrobiotic Source Books	210
Bibliography	212
Glossary	213
Index	215

Foreword

LAST SUMMER, the author brought the manuscript of this book to the Macrobiotic summer camp which was held at Tahoe National Forest in California. I read it with great pleasure and advised her on a few corrections. In my opinion, it is the best and most comprehensive introduction to macrobiotic cooking that has been written in English. Its information is practical, yet it never overlooks the importance of the macrobiotic principle underlying the cooking. The explanation of cooking techniques is simple and to the point, describing clearly the many aspects of macrobiotic cooking that beginners will encounter, including kitchenwares, foodstuffs, condiments, and even nutritional theory from the macrobiotic point of view.

Recently, my wife and I made a tour of the United States and Canada, lecturing on macrobiotics and giving cooking lessons to over a thousand people. It is evident that interest in macrobiotics is growing, and that the demand for a thorough introductory cookbook is urgent.

At this time, Eunice Farmilant's book will be like a spring found in the middle of a desert. I wholeheartedly recommend it to all those who want to take up macrobiotic cooking as well as to those who have been doing it for years.

HERMAN AIHARA
President, George Ohsawa
Macrobiotic Foundation
San Francisco, California

Introduction

MACROBIOTIC COOKING, developed by George Ohsawa and based upon traditional ideas of culinary art, is a method of food preparation with higher goals than just those of simple health. It is a cooking method that is backed by a total philosophy, representing hundreds of years of Eastern and Western thought. The basic ideas of macrobiotics can be applied to any race in any country. The principles, when applied to foods, result in a diet that is very inexpensive, with a great deal of variety, delicious to eat, and simple to prepare. It is food fit for a peasant or a king.

The underlying ideas of macrobiotic cosmology relate to spiritual health and happiness as well as physical well-being. Macrobiotic cooking is the first step toward the attainment of all three. This book is an introduction to cooking and eating as part of the macrobiotic way of life.

If you are curious about macrobiotics, read the book, try several of the recipes, and see what happens. Many of the recipes presented here formed the basis of cooking classes I have given. For those of you who want to know more about the philosophy behind macrobiotics I have listed a bibliography at the end of this book. Also included (on p. 213) is a glossary of foods used in macrobiotic cooking which may be unfamiliar to the reader.

Macrobiotic Cooking

How I Got into Macrobiotics

ONE NIGHT IN APRIL, 1968, my brother Stephen went to a lecture on macrobiotics given in Chicago. He was so impressed by what he saw and heard that he took my father with him to attend another lecture the next night.

My father had been a health food faddist for years, and for over a decade the entire family had had to endure with him almost every dietary phase. However, this new interest, fostered on the night of that lecture, appeared to be somewhat different. His enthusiasm didn't subside after just a few weeks, and during the next six months he would come to my apartment bearing small loaves of bread he had baked and leave sacks of brown rice, millet, or aduki beans on my kitchen table.

In the summer my brother moved to Boston to study with Michio Kushi, the lecturer he had heard that spring. I soon began receiving letters from him describing the joys of eating "according to the order of the universe," each accompanied by articles taken from various magazines and illustrated with little triangles which supposedly symbolized "yin" and "yang." I was puzzled by this language and began to think my brother had flipped out.

By November of that year I had read all the George Ohsawa books on macrobiotics that my father had lent me, as well as a small cookbook called *Zen Cookery* which I regarded more as a work of science fiction than a basic guidebook to natural eating. I was busy with school, my job, an active social life, and my friends. I found the literature interesting, even startling, but I was too involved with personal interests to want to do something as drastic as changing my eating habits of twenty-two years.

In December I had a four-week semester break and just as an experiment decided to begin the diet. Within a month

I had permanently given up coffee, sugar, artificial foods, most dairy products, and meat—in short, the standard American diet. By January I was hooked.

Early in May of 1969 I attended a lecture and saw William Dufty, the author of *You Are All Sanpaku*. I found him an amusing, attractive man who looked about thirty-five or forty. His informal conversation was lively and the joy he generated was contagious. Then he told us his age. He was fifty-four!

That evening I suddenly realized that the philosophy presented in macrobiotics was exactly what I was searching for. Two weeks later I was on a plane bound for Boston to study more about macrobiotics. I had quit school, my job, given up my apartment, and said good-bye to all my friends. My life had changed.

Macrobiotics is more than just a diet. It's a whole way of life. To try to describe how much it can change you is like trying to verbalize a state of ecstasy. However, it is not by any means a "miracle diet" but rather a well-structured set of principles that lay a groundwork for health. Weight loss, more energy, and generally more positive feelings are some of the more noticeable changes produced by macrobiotics. But there is a vast network of other more subtle changes that may continue to surprise you for years. And the longer you continue with the diet, the more your appetite for everything in life will change, as your body and mind adjust to physical and spiritual harmony.

The Meaning of Macrobiotics

LITERALLY TRANSLATED from the Greek, "macrobiotics" means big life. However, the meaning of the word as applied to living is different for each one of us. Forced to define a single principle behind the philosophy of the macrobiotic diet, one could say it means choosing and eating those foods grown within approximately a five-hundred-mile radius of one's home, and living in accord with one's immediate environment.

In extremely cold climates, where vegetation was scarce and animal products abundant, man adjusted to his harsh environment by eating animal food almost exclusively—the only food source around. In hot, tropical climates man ate those foods native to his surroundings. This was the natural order.

Today, modern methods of cultivation, processing, preserving, and distribution make it possible for someone living in Alaska to enjoy strawberries in January, while someone in Florida can dine on caribou meat in July. The natural order of eating has disappeared.

The enormous variety of food we can choose from is a luxury we are fortunate to have. However, we must learn to choose properly from these foods in order to maintain a sense of balance in our bodies and harmony with our surroundings. This involves eating with a purpose by selecting foods best suited to our daily activities, nutritional and biological needs, our climate, and our general well-being. In this sense, the principles of macrobiotics take all of life into consideration to insure the best possible diet for everyone's particular needs.

Yin and Yang

YIN AND YANG are two Chinese words used to express the idea of polarity, the antagonistic aspects of the "oneness" of the universe. Everything contains yin and yang—the classification only comes into consideration when something has more "yin" or more "yang" as compared to something else. Everything in the world is in a state of constant change between these two forces. Ideally, through macrobiotics we strive to create a balance in order to achieve a state of oneness with the universe.

Confused? Yin and yang are not new ideas, nor are they new terms; they are simply a way of looking at the world around us with a different understanding. Yin is expansive, with an outward centrifugal tendency. Yang is contracting, inward, a centripetal tendency. Night is yin; it is cool and dark, a time when our activity slows down and silence prevails. Daytime is yang, warmer, a time when we are more active physically, talk louder, and tend not to concern ourselves with the same thoughts that enter our minds at night.

Men are yang; women are more passive and yin. A baby is very yang at birth; small and contracted, he is hungry all the time and grows rapidly. As he grows older he becomes more yin, until finally, before death, he again becomes contracted and dies. Yin and yang continually seek their opposites.

If we compare the seasons, winter is yin, cold and dark. We seek the comfort of our homes, we eat food that makes us more yang, that is, more animal products, root vegetables, and salt. Summer is yang; the hot sun attracts us to green leafy vegetables, we are lured outside and tend to lose our taste for heavy dishes and salty foods.

To fully understand yin and yang is a lifelong process. To develop an understanding of these terms as applied to daily cooking takes time, but they will become more natural once you begin to cook with these ideas in mind.

Looking at our food from a chemical viewpoint, sodium is yang, potassium, yin. To achieve a balance between these two elements in cooking, we try to maintain a ratio of five to seven parts potassium to one part sodium. This ratio is maintained in our blood; it can be traced back to seawater, the beginning fluid of life. Whole brown rice is considered the most balanced grain. If we were able to eat nothing but brown rice the balance would perhaps be maintained constantly. Rice is a wonderful food, but at present our bodies are unable to absorb everything from one particular food to meet all our nutritional needs. And according to the principles of macrobiotics there is no need to eat one food exclusively—we have the freedom to choose any foods we want—provided we balance them to maintain harmony.

The average diet of many people consists of large quantities of meat and sugar. This is a form of balance, but it is achieved through the use of extremes. Meat is very yang, sugar very yin. Our bodies must strain continually to maintain the slightly alkaloid ratio in our blood and, in doing so, are sometimes forced to remove stored minerals from body tissues. Eventually we take the risk of depleting our mineral reserves, weakening our bones and vitality. This state comes about when our blood becomes too acid from eating too much yin food.

Of course, taking pleasure in eating is important. Foods that beckon all the senses—sunlight, clean air and water—help to keep us happy and healthy. But we eat for more important reasons than pleasure alone—to provide energy, material for growth, and to maintain our bodies. All nutritive elements come from the vegetable world which transforms the basic chemicals into digestible food forms. If we allow these substances to be absorbed by animals, and then eat animal meat, we run the risk of these elements becoming altered and unbalanced, separated, partly concentrated, full of toxic wastes and the putrefactive bacteria of decomposition. (I won't even talk about the artificial chemicals man has given to animals in the form of vaccines, drugs, and antibiotics.)

A macrobiotic diet is not a strict vegetarian diet, but a system of eating as few animal foods as possible. The animal foods recommended are those that come from lower forms of life, such as shellfish, wild game birds, eggs, or fish: in other words, animals that have been the least tampered with by man. You can, however, eat a vegetarian diet and be macrobiotic. A mixed diet of grains, vegetables, beans, fruit, and nuts *can* supply all the vitamins and minerals we need, sugars and starches for energy, fats, oils, and proteins (including essential amino acids) for body building and tissue repair. The addition of animal products is a compromise with man's desire for other foods.

During the past several hundred years, we have become heavy meat-eaters. This has not been a sudden switch from grains and vegetables, but a gradual one. The same pattern must be repeated when we decide to reverse our eating habits. Therefore, it is wise to cut down on animal foods gradually, substituting chicken, fish, and cheese for red meat while adjusting to whole grains. This prevents the body from being subjected to sudden shocks. Elimination of other foods, including chemically treated products, sugar, and drugs, should be attempted from the beginning, by substituting "real food," i.e., fresh vegetables and fruits, and only those foods which have been dried or processed naturally.

Here is a list for classifying foods according to yin and yang.*

	Yin	Yang
Color†	purple	red
Direction of Growth	up	down
Element	potassium	sodium
Growth Tendency	outward	inward
Biological	vegetable	animal
Agricultural	salad	cereal
Season of Growth	summer	fall, winter
Taste	sweet, sour, spicy	salty, bitter
Vitamin	C	A, D, K
Where Grown	tropical climate	temperate climate
Weight	light	heavy
Water Content	high (juicy)	low (dry)

* See pp. 187–188 for individual listing of foods according to yin/yang.
† *Yin*—high frequency vibration
purple—   blue violet—   yellow— green—   green red—
(eggplant) (purple cabbage) (corn) (kale)   (dandelion greens)
red-orange—
(carrot)
Yang—low frequency vibration
red
(aduki beans)

Eating Whole Foods

THE IDEA of eating foods in a whole, natural state has almost completely vanished from our modern-day understanding of food. Eating only part of an apple, a carrot, or a grain of rice, and discarding the rest is a way of robbing ourselves of the full value of our food, as well as being wasteful from an ecological viewpoint. The most vivid example of this can be seen in a glass of extracted fruit or vegetable juice. The food is whirled in a machine that breaks down the cellular structure, extracts the juice and the pulp. The end product that we consume contains the juice, minus the plant fibers. What have we thrown away? The roughage that helps to keep our intestines active as well as a lot of other valuable nutrients left in the pulp. Not only that, but vitamins have been lost through the extraction process, and the longer the time lapse between processing and consumption, the greater the chance of further loss. Moreover, we lose the opportunity to chew and to exercise facial muscles, which can become lax through lack of use.

Grains are the most perfectly balanced foods when eaten whole. The outer layers of a grain contain minerals and vitamins, while the inner core is made up mostly of carbohydrates. Since the outer layer aids in digesting the carbohydrate, milling and further processing of grain removes this necessary substance and an incomplete food is the result. In macrobiotics, the idea is to use foods in roughly the same proportions as they are found in nature, and to use them in the most natural state possible. In temperate climates where grains are the most abundant foods, and are native to the terrain, they should therefore make up a large proportion of our diet.

Why We Cook Our Foods

MAN is the only animal who has the choice of preparing his food in a way that is best for his physical and spiritual development. Cooking is actually the first step in digestion. We cook food for many reasons—to improve taste and aroma and also to break down the cellulose walls in order to release elements stored in the plant cells. Man has cooked his food for thousands of years in almost every part of the world.

Today many vegetarians and raw-food eaters argue that cooking destroys the nutritional value of foods by killing vitamins and other essential elements. This claim is partly true, for many methods of food preparation do cause great losses in food value. However, there are cooking methods that preserve the essential nutrients, and in the case of macrobiotics, food values can actually be improved.

Macrobiotics uses the same basic elements in preparing food that man has used throughout his development—fire, salt, pressure, and time. Using these four forces all together or in various combinations we can prepare our food through baking, boiling, pickling, pressure cooking, sautéing, deep-frying, or steaming. All of the conventional cooking methods are described in detail throughout the recipe section of this volume, but first let's go over the four forces again in terms of yin and yang.

Fire

When man discovered fire, civilization began. Man is the only animal on earth who has learned how to control fire. He has the ability to release the energy of the plant world without converting it first into body fuel as do animals who carry the stored energy of the plant world within them to maintain their body heat.

At first, man used wood, a relatively low-energy (yang) fuel to cook his food and keep his house warm. As he progressed, he discovered the more powerful fuels—coal, oil, gas, and finally electricity and atomic fuel (very yin).

Because of the enormous demand for high-energy (yin) fuels, such as electricity, very few people today depend upon the low-energy fuels, such as coal or wood.

We use fire to neutralize the acid content of yin (vegetable quality) food in order to extract the yang qualities.

Salt

For better health and taste, unrefined white sea salt is the best quality salt to use in cooking. This salt has been sun-dried and contains all the trace minerals left after seawater has been evaporated—magnesium, calcium, phosphorus, and iron as well as trace amounts of iodine. Supermarket varieties of table salt have been refined and baked at high temperatures in kilns. Through heating, purifying, and filtering, all that remains of this natural product is sodium chloride, plus a few other trace amounts of poisonous compounds that have been added to prevent the salt from caking.

Because it is unrefined, sea salt must be dry-roasted in a skillet over a medium flame for at least 10 minutes with occasional stirring in order to drive off the excess chlorine. While roasting the salt, if you lean over the pan and sniff, you can smell the chlorine gas escaping. When the salt turns slightly brown and the smell diminishes, turn off the flame and let the pan cool thoroughly before storing the salt in an airtight container. Do not use any lids that have a rubber ring—the salt will completely erode the rubber over a short period of time. Only small quantities of salt need to be roasted at a time; it should be used sparingly in cooking.

WHY WE COOK OUR FOODS 29

Although the primary seasoning in our cooking is sea salt, *miso*, *tamari*, and *umeboshi* (salt plums)* are all excellent sources of salt and can be used in place of sea salt in many recipes.

Several very important things about salt must be remembered in macrobiotic cooking. Salt helps to balance oil. The ideal ratio is one part salt to five parts oil. That is why we use more salt when deep-frying or using foods rich in oil to create a balance. The salt also greatly aids in the digestion of oil.

There are two major ways in which salt can affect our bodies. One is the physical contraction caused when one eats a lot of salt and drinks very little liquid. The other is the physical expansion caused by eating a lot of salt, and also drinking a lot of water, for if we eat a lot of salt and drink a great deal of liquid the salt will retain the water, resulting in a bloated state. This is a very vivid example, somewhat simplified, of how yin and yang work.

As you begin macrobiotic cooking, try to use less salt than you normally would for regular cooking. Since we have eaten large quantities of meat our bodies are already full of sodium.

The importance of salt cannot be over-stressed. To find out the exact amount of salt that is right for you takes a good deal of experimenting. Too little salt can lead to fatigue, whereas too much salt also creates undesirable side effects such as tension, a rigid feeling, and inability to sleep well.

Whenever possible, add salt during cooking, not afterward. Adding salt during cooking alters foods and makes it easier for the body to digest them and absorb the sodium. Generally, grain preparations are made with very little salt and taste quite sweet, while vegetable side dishes are made much saltier, and serve as a garnish to complement our main foods.

Sesame Salt or Gomasio

Sesame salt, also called gomasio, is used in place of plain salt as a seasoning agent on the table in macrobiotic homes. This condiment is a mixture of roasted sesame seeds and sea salt which have been ground together so that about 80

* See Glossary, p. 213.

percent of the seeds are crushed. The ratio of sea salt to seeds varies according to individual tastes and needs, but a good proportion to start out with is one part salt to ten or fifteen parts seeds. Grind roasted sea salt in a suribachi (a serrated ceramic mortar, see illustration, p. 43) until it becomes a fine powder. Wash the sesame seeds thoroughly in a fine strainer. About one cup of sesame seeds should be sufficient for a week's supply of gomasio for two people. Dry-roast the seeds over a medium flame in a heavy skillet on the top of the stove for about 15 minutes. Stir constantly with chopsticks or a wooden spoon to prevent burning. Shake the pan occasionally to distribute the seeds. When they are light brown and give off a distinctive fragrance, they will begin to pop and should be removed from the heat.

Grind the seeds into the salt, holding the wooden pestle upright in one hand while using the other to support the bowl firmly in your lap. Stirring in a counter-clockwise direction, grind slowly from the center. Store in a clean, airtight glass container. Gomasio takes time to prepare, so be sure to make it when you are not in a hurry to cook dinner. The oil of the sesame seeds coats the salt, creating a delicate seasoning that adds extra flavor to all foods. Try a little on everything—it's even good on watermelon.

Time and Pressure

These two yang factors are combined together in various ways when we prepare foods. For example, pickles or pressed salad, while not cooked over direct heat, become yangized through the use of salt. A weight is then placed on top of the pickling container, or else water (a brine solution) is added. The combination of salt, long periods of time, and pressure are yang factors which serve to neutralize excess acidity in vegetables, draw out excess liquid, and also to some extent break down the cellular structure. In regular cooking, the pressure created by the steam within a covered pot bears down upon the foods. With a pressure cooker this force is many times greater.

We try to keep these ideas of cooking in mind when we prepare foods. Just as the seasons change, so must our methods of cooking change with them. In winter, the season is yin, and our cooking is more yang—more pressure, more salt—we tend to like foods cooked longer, etc. In summer the season is yang, and we can adopt lighter methods of cooking—less pressure-cooking, more lightly cooked foods, pressed salads, and less salt.

The understanding of how to apply these very basic ideas to cooking is the key to balanced macrobiotic cooking. It is more than merely culinary expertise—for it involves taking all of the environmental factors that surround us into consideration when we prepare our foods. What we eat today will affect our actions tomorrow. When we begin to see this not merely as printed words but as part of our experience we begin to understand what true macrobiotic cooking means.

Stocking Your Kitchen

MAKING THE SWITCH from the standard American diet to macrobiotics is a pretty big step. If you've been on a modified vegetarian diet (many of us who got interested in macrobiotics studied yoga and were into dairy products, fresh fruits, and vegetables, etc.), the switch is not so sudden. The best approach is a gradual one, and the following items provide a flexible variety of foods that can be your staples, or can be used along with the foods you are reluctant to give up at first.

Although the food cost may seem high at first, especially if you are buying in small quantities and are continuing to eat expensive animal products, after a few weeks you'll be amazed at how cheap simple natural foods are. Prices do fluctuate according to season and area; I've found in New York City, for instance, wide price differences between one store and another. However, our food bill for two adults usually averages between ten and fifteen dollars a week. If you are fortunate enough to have some land available for a vegetable garden or can buy in large quantities, food should only cost a few dollars per person per week.

If there are no macrobiotic stores near you, write to any of the stores or distributors listed at the end of this book. Then you can order your staples by mail, supplementing other items through health food stores. Or perhaps you can organize a group of people who are interested in eating this way and form a cooperative to order wholesale.

For two adults just starting on the diet the following list may be used as a rough guide for buying enough food to last a few weeks.

Basics

Short-grain brown rice—Short-grain rice is the best variety to buy. The grains should be small, uniform in size and color. Organic brown rice is now available, but is not carried by all macrobiotic sources. It is much cheaper to buy rice in large quantities (100-pound bags), but in the beginning you can start out with a modest ten or fifteen pounds.

Bancha tea—This is Japanese green tea, undyed and pure. It is the most essential beverage of the macrobiotic diet and contains about three times more calcium than cow's milk. It is not only delicious, but also economical; each tablespoon of roasted leaves will make a full pot and the leaves can be used several times. About four ounces is a generous amount to begin with.

Miso paste—Traditional soybean miso paste is a high-protein concentrated food used as a flavoring agent in many dishes and as a base for soup stocks. It has a salty, almost meatlike taste and a chocolate texture. There are several varieties to choose from. Hacho is the strongest; it is a dark chocolate brown and very salty, and is used mainly in the winter. Mugi is a lighter miso made with barley. It is fine for year-round use and much better in summer than hacho. Kome is the lightest of all miso; it is made with rice and less salt. It is best for summer use and good for children and older adults. Begin with a two-pound package of mugi miso.*

Beans—Aduki beans are the most yang beans; they are similar in structure to grains. This variety is very high in protein and also has a unique flavor. Buy just one pound at first; other good beans to try are black beans, chickpeas, and lentils.

Seaweeds—Seaweed is one food that most people are hesitant to try. This sea vegetable is found in many shapes, sizes, and varieties. Most people find hiziki, a black, stringy seaweed, most palatable. It generally comes in three-and-a-half-ounce packages, but some stores carry it loose so you can buy any quantity you desire. An ounce of seaweed goes a long way, especially a variety such as hiziki which must be soaked before cooking.

Nori is another good seaweed to try. It comes packaged

---

* For more information on miso, see p. 142ff.

34 STOCKING YOUR KITCHEN

in thin sheets and only needs to be lightly toasted over a burner.

Other grains—For variety, and until you feel more at ease with preparing whole grain, try a few pounds of buckwheat groats (less in hot weather), a couple of pounds of millet and rolled oats.

Flour—For making breads, pancakes, and sauces, you'll need about five pounds of whole wheat flour, one or two pounds of corn flour, a pound of rice flour, and one pound of buckwheat. As flour does not stay fresh over long periods of time (oxidation, which leads to rancidity, begins within 16 hours after grain is milled), it is best to buy in small quantities. Later on, you'll probably want to invest in a grain mill (they retail for about $12) so that you can enjoy fresh flour all the time.

Oil—Natural, unrefined sesame, corn germ, soya, or sunflower oils are recommended for the best results in cooking and baking. They are more expensive than supermarket varieties, but since they are used sparingly the prices are reasonable. Start out with a pint of sesame or sunflower and another pint of corn germ or soya oil.

Fresh vegetables and fruits—Ideally, one should get organically grown vegetables. If these naturally fertilized, unsprayed foods are beyond your means at least try to use those vegetables that are in season and scrub the skins thoroughly. Because most supermarket fruits and many vegetables are waxed to improve their shelf life (keeping qualities), it's best to peel them.

Dried fruits, nuts, and seeds—Dried apples, currants, raisins, sesame and sunflower seeds, almonds, and walnuts are handy for making desserts and satisfying when you want a snack. Avoid fruits that are chemically dried with sulfur dioxide—sun-dried varieties are available in all health food stores, natural food shops, and macrobiotic food outlets.

Condiments

Tamari soy sauce*—Another soybean product made from pure ingredients and aged for about eighteen months. Indis-

---

* Tamari is a brand name for traditional Japanese soy sauce, and is frequently used throughout the book in place of the words soy sauce to avoid confusion with most commercial non-macrobiotic brands. Traditional soy sauce can also be found under the name of lima soy sauce.

pensable as a seasoning agent and table condiment, it contains 6 percent protein and has a strong, salty taste. A quart will last two people one month.

Salted plums (umeboshi)—These plums are aged in a salt solution for about two years. Some come with chiso leaves; chiso is a plant native to Japan and contains a natural dye which lends a bright orange color to the fruit. Plums are used for flavoring in sauces, with rice, salads, and vegetables. Start out with an eight-ounce jar.

Sea salt—Unrefined white sea salt is used exclusively in macrobiotic cooking because of the natural presence of trace minerals and iodine. It must be roasted first to remove excess chlorine. One pound will last about a year. Sea salt is much stronger than plain table salt.

Sesame salt—Sesame salt (gomasio) is used in place of table salt in macrobiotic homes. It is a delicate, tasty seasoning that goes well with everything. Although it does come commercially prepared, it is best to make your own at home, using a suribachi (serrated ceramic mortar). More detailed directions are given on p. 29.

Miscellaneous Food Items

Agar-agar—A sea vegetable with gelatinous properties, used as a thickening agent in desserts.

Apple butter—Pure organic apple butter is fine to use occasionally.

Arrowroot starch—A pure white thickening agent, preferred to corn starch because it is not chemically processed; arrowroot is used in sauces, soups, desserts, etc.

Crackers—Readymade organic products are handy for snacks; most natural food stores carry corn or rice varieties.

Mu tea—A sixteen-herb beverage, mu tea is a strong, fragrant brew that can be served occasionally in place of bancha tea. For more information on other teas, see beverage section.

Noodles—Pure grain products made without eggs; buckwheat and whole wheat noodles (both come in macaroni and spaghetti forms) offer a pleasing variety.

Peanut butter—Organic peanut butter made from roasted peanuts is fine to use once in a while as a supplemental food. However, peanuts are actually beans and, because of their high concentrations of starch, oil, and protein, are sometimes difficult to digest.

36 STOCKING YOUR KITCHEN

Organic popcorn—Try making it with corn oil and using sesame salt or tamari to flavor it.

Tiny dried fish—Found in macrobiotic outlets, these fish, also known as <u>chirimen iriko</u>, can be used to flavor soup stocks, or may be ground up in a suribachi and eaten as a condiment with rice and vegetables.

Tofu—A soybean curd product. Tofu is carried in Oriental food shops; however, you may prefer to make your own according to the directions given in the section on beans.

Spices—Although tropical foods and strong spices are almost entirely excluded from a macrobiotic diet, there is still room for a touch of bay leaf, basil, cinnamon, garlic, ginger, oregano, thyme, or vanilla bean to accent or spike a meal.

Storing of Food

VERY LITTLE of the food you will be buying needs to be refrigerated. Refrigeration has a very yinizing effect—it is cold, damp, and dark, besides the fact that it is operated by electricity. Only highly perishable vegetables and fruits or animal products and foods that decompose easily *need* to be placed in a refrigerator.

Grain—If you buy in large quantities the grain can be left in its original burlap sack, which allows for air circulation. Place in a cool, dry area. However, if you have any pets be sure to keep the grain off the floor—cats and dogs are often attracted to burlap!

Otherwise, large, wide-mouth glass jars are excellent storage containers. They are attractive enough to sit on display anywhere in the kitchen. Just be sure to keep them away from artificial heat or direct sunlight. Properly stored, whole grain can keep for several years.

Flour—Because flour is no longer the whole grain (milling breaks up the germ and protective outer layers) it begins to lose its properties rapidly and should never be kept for long periods of time. Store flour in glass jars in a dark, cool place. Lightly roasting the stored flour in a dry skillet before using it in cooking will sweeten the taste.

Miso—Neither miso nor tamari soy sauce should ever be refrigerated—just store them in a pantry. Occasionally a white crust may form on the top of the miso, or the tamari may develop a white deposit; both of these are natural occurrences so don't worry, just mix the whitish material back into the miso or tamari. Large quantities of miso come in kegs—

these are useful for making pickles (see section on pickles for details). Smaller quantities often come in plastic bags and you may prefer to transfer the contents to a glass jar.

Vegetables, beans, nuts, seeds, dried fruit, seaweed, etc.—All can be kept in a cool place. A pantry with an open window is the ideal storage room, the next best place is an enclosed porch. Except for highly perishable vegetables, most fresh vegetables and fruits will keep well if stored this way for several days or a week. Wilted vegetables are perfectly good to use—they are just a bit dehydrated. Root vegetables can be stored for longer periods of time (several months) when buried in boxes of sand or sawdust.

Condiments—Keep a small supply of roasted sea salt, tamari, sesame seeds, and oil near the stove so they will always be handy.

Leftovers—Cooked grains keep very well without refrigeration even during the summer. However, grains that have been slightly processed, like bulgar and couscous or cracked cereals, break down and ferment more quickly. When storing cooked food don't cover the container too tightly because this will speed up fermentation by cutting off the air supply. Cooked rice keeps best in a wooden bowl with a light bamboo mat (found in Oriental gift shops) for a lid. During hot weather an umeboshi salt plum or two placed in the bowl will keep rice fresh longer. Sometimes a bright orange mold may form over rice when the weather is particularly humid—just scrape it off and the rice will be all right to use. Grain that has gone sour is good for making bread doughs, muffins, pancakes, etc.

Sautéed vegetables, soup, seaweed, etc., all can be kept overnight or longer in cold weather without refrigeration. Place in earthenware or glass containers. Avoid metal and plastic containers—they often leave a faint taste in the food.

Stored grain and condiments can be placed on shelves in the kitchen.

A windowsill is a good place to store utensils.

Potted chives and carrot tops add a decorative touch besides being handy for salads.

Utensils Are Your Basic Tools

PROPER UTENSILS are the basic tools for happy cooking. Although one pot is all you really need to make a simple meal, for convenience during preparation it helps to have some accessory items. The most important investment in macrobiotic cooking is a pressure cooker, made out of stainless steel or porcelain enamel. A good pressure cooker is an expensive investment initially, but properly cared for it will last many years.

Try to select cookware and serving items made of natural materials that do not impart any flavor, and those materials that harmonize with the foods. Cookware made out of more yang materials—such as earthenware, cast-iron, baked enamel (over cast-iron), are preferred over the yin manmade items, such as aluminum, Teflon, copper, and tin alloys.

Also, try to get into the habit of using wooden implements when handling food during cooking. Wood never scratches pots or pans and does not injure vegetables during cooking.

I've used the following items in my kitchen for the past three years, and have only had to make very minor investments for items lost or damaged during moving. When I started macrobiotic cooking my first pressure cooker was a secondhand cast-aluminum gem, about ten years old and missing the regulator and gasket. It was a gift from my brother. I learned to make a lot of things with it, and used it until I could afford to buy a stainless steel model. If you're on a budget and not terribly fussy, secondhand stores, flea markets, and thrift shops often carry some terrific kitchen bargains. My favorite pot is a cast-iron dutch oven I bought for two dollars at a flea market in Chicago.

Basic Items

Asbestos pad—Several of these are handy to have in the kitchen. They can be found in hardware stores, dime stores, and special culinary shops. Placed between the flame and the bottom of the pan, they prevent scorch marks and keep food from sticking and burning. They are very inexpensive.

Cast-iron skillets—For sautéing, frying, dry-roasting grains, seeds, or nuts, cast-iron skillets are indispensable items. Purchased new or secondhand, they are relatively inexpensive and will last a lifetime. To season a new skillet, cook some salt in it until it becomes discolored (to absorb the protective wax covering). Let cool, then wash in plain water. Sauté an onion in the skillet with plenty of oil for about 30 minutes. This will remove the iron taste.

Chopping block—For longer wear, be sure to get a block at least one inch thick and free of glaze or varnish. Hardwood maple is the best wood. Always wash your board with cold water after use to keep it fresh.

Chopping knife—A heavy Japanese knife with a squared-off end is the perfect all-purpose knife. They cost anywhere from three to six dollars, depending on size and weight. The best ones are made of carbon steel, have a sturdy wooden handle, and will last a couple of years.

Chopsticks—We use chopsticks in place of metal implements for eating simply because we prefer the taste of bamboo to metal. Also, for stirring food during cooking, several pairs of long cooking chopsticks are handy. These are the Chinese variety and are carried in Oriental shops and many macrobiotic food stores.

Graters—The flat graters are best; try to get stainless steel or porcelain graters that have a fine section for grating daikon (white radish) or ginger root.

Hand grain mill—If you're concerned about eating the freshest flours, a grain mill is a relatively inexpensive investment that pays for itself in a short time. A grain mill can also be used for making nut and seed butters, crushed nuts, and cracked cereals. It adds a very homey touch to your kitchen.

Oil strainer—A fine mesh strainer used for removing

vegetables when making tempura. Chopsticks will usually do the job, but the strainer makes things a little easier.

Pastry brush—Helps save time and prevents using extra oil. You can also use a nylon paintbrush or a goose feather.

Pressure cooker—Porcelain or stainless steel is recommended over plain or cast aluminum. Be sure to replace parts periodically.

Pyrex coffeepot—Glass makes the best material for a teapot—it doesn't impart or absorb odors and is easy to keep clean.

Rice paddle—Made of bamboo, this cheap utilitarian implement, available in Oriental stores, is handy for anything that needs mixing or stirring and is also great for serving. To prevent rice from sticking to the paddle, rinse in cold water before use.

Saucepans—Depending upon the number of people you're cooking for, one or two one-and-a-half-quart pans are usually sufficient. Heavy saucepans retain heat best and allow for more even cooking.

Soup pot—A large, heavy pot made of cast iron or porcelain or steel with a tight-fitting lid is all that is necessary for making soup and noodles, or for steaming vegetables. If you are fortunate enough to own two pressure cookers, one can usually be used as a soup pot.

Soy sauce dispenser—A small glass container with a special spout that can be found in macrobiotic foodstores and Oriental shops. For table use, or cooking.

Suribachi—A ridged earthenware mortar used for grinding sesame salt, making purees, etc.

Vegetable brush (*tawashi*)—A natural fiber brush for scrubbing vegetables. Found in macrobiotic stores and Oriental shops.

Wok—A Chinese cooking pot perfect for tempura (deep frying) and all kinds of fast cooking. Found in department and Oriental stores.

Wooden spoons—All shapes and sizes are good for stirring, mixing, and serving.

Miscellaneous

Foley food mill—For making purees, creaming desserts and vegetables.

Mesh strainer—For washing grains, seeds, etc.

UTENSILS ARE YOUR BASIC TOOLS 43

Tea strainer—Bamboo is aesthetically appealing; stainless steel is also good.

Colander—For washing vegetables, rinsing noodles.

Baking equipment—One or two bread pans, Pyrex or stainless steel; a cookie sheet; pie pans, casserole dishes (with covers), cake pans.

soup pot

cast-iron skillet

grater

suribachi

wooden spoons

chopsticks

vegetable brush

pressure cooker

chopping knife

strainer

wok

Some Notes on Your Utensils

You'll soon discover that vegetable oils are easier to clean than animal fats, and consequently dishwashing becomes a simple matter of using warm running water. Any detergent or cleanser used in washing goes into the surface pores of your pots and pans, not to mention what it does to the environment. It is therefore better to avoid harsh chemical detergents and use a biodegradable soap (made of organic matter) for general cleaning.

If a pot has some burned food stuck to the bottom, soak it overnight in plain tap water. In the morning all cooked foods will become loose enough to remove with a wooden spoon or sponge. This way you can avoid scouring with steel wool which damages the finish and decreases the life of your utensils.

A suribachi is easy to clean if it is rinsed immediately after use and whisked lightly with a brush. Invert over a burner to dry out thoroughly before storing in a cupboard.

To prevent rust, always dry cast-iron pots over the burner on a low flame after washing. Re-season surface occasionally, using a small amount of oil after cleaning, and heat over a low flame for 20 to 30 minutes.

Place all wooden utensils (chopsticks, spoons, etc.) in a large container upside down to dry.

Vitamins, Minerals, Proteins, etc.

As LONG as we maintain a balanced diet of cereal grains, fresh vegetables, seaweeds, beans, and small amounts of fruit and animal food (if we desire it), all the essential matter needed for health will be present in abundance. There is no need to take any food supplements or vitamins when everything you need is already there. All supplements are extractions, whether they are called "organic" or synthetic, and at best are an unnatural means of taking in needed nutrients. Just how much the body is able to absorb from artificially condensed food supplements is the subject of much debate and remains a medical enigma.

This section will discuss food values, comparing one food to another. Hopefully, it will satisfy any doubts you may have about the nutritional value of a macrobiotic diet. If you aren't terribly concerned about scientific evidence, and are content to follow the principles of macrobiotics purely by intuition, this chapter may be skipped. However, the collection of simple charts and tables can be useful in verifying any statements made in this book concerning the basic laws of nutrition.

It must be pointed out that improper cooking, soaking certain foods for long periods of time prior to preparation (see chart on vitamin loss in cooking), and carelessness in handling often destroy the vitamin and mineral content of many foods. Therefore, even if you are eating the finest organically grown foods, if you don't know how to prepare them in the most advantageous fashion, much of the natural goodness will be lost. Try to be aware of everything you do when preparing food in order to make the most of it.

Vitamins

All the vitamin propaganda we hear today sounds quite convincing; if we skip meals or diet, a few pills will help keep things in order—or do they? Vitamin pills often do help somewhat, but over a period of time their effectiveness diminishes. We have within our bodies a marvelously complex chemical laboratory, capable of creating the most puzzling chemical formulas that scientists do not entirely understand. Provided that our bodies are given the raw materials, and are functioning at their best, they even have the ability to create vitamins. It is the poor physical condition of many people that has made them unable to make their own vitamins. If you eat heavily processed foods, or foods that are frozen, canned, dehydrated, or whatever other mutilation vegetable and animal products are so often subjected to, vitamin pills should probably also be a regular part of your diet.

By choosing well, we can still get all the essential vitamins in our daily diet. The chart on the next page shows the best food sources, and the vitamins are arranged from yang to yin. If you notice the chemical formula of the vitamins, you can see that those which are most yang have a high percentage of hydrogen and low amounts of oxygen. This balance is reversed in the yin vitamins. Yang foods are also more contracted than the expanded yin vegetables.

The amount of vitamin C found in green leafy vegetables is more than twice the amount found in citrus fruits. If you are eating a balanced diet of vegetables, grains, seaweeds, beans, and fruits you will never have to worry about developing vitamin deficiencies.

Minerals

Minerals play an active role in building body tissue and are especially essential in the proper functioning of the entire nervous system and body metabolism. Calcium, phosphorus, and magnesium are some of the most important minerals and are found in seaweeds, nuts, and green vegetables. Sesame seeds are a good source of iron. Deep green leafy vegetables and seaweed are excellent sources of iodine.

VITAMINS FOUND IN THE FOODS WE EAT

Food Quality	Vitamin Name and Formula	Recommended Allowance for Adults	Best Sources	Other Good Sources
Yang	K—antihemorrhagic $C_{31}H_{46}O_2$	About 0.5 mg.	Green leafy vegetables	Unrefined oils, brown rice, also produced by the intestinal flora
	D—$C_{28}H_{44}O$	400 I.U.	Sunlight	Dried fish, some vegetables
	E—antisterility $C_{29}H_{50}O_2$	10–30 I.U.	Cereal grains, wheat, brown rice	Nuts, legumes, green leafy vegetables
	A—retinol $C_{20}H_{30}O$	5000 I.U.	Dandelion greens—14,000 I.U.; carrots—11,000; kale—10,000	Parsley, watercress, spinach
	B_2—riboflavin $C_{17}H_{17}N_4O_6$	1.0–1.6 mg.	Sunflower seeds—1.96 mg.; rice bran—2.26 mg.; soybeans—1.10 mg.	Peanuts, pinto beans, millet, wheat, rye, sesame seeds
	B_1—thiamine $C_{12}H_{17}ClN_4OS·HCL$	1.5–1.8 mg.	Almonds—0.92 mg.; kelp—0.33 mg.; soybeans—0.31 mg.	Brown rice, beans, lentils
	C—ascorbic acid $C_6H_8O_6$	70–75 mg.	Parsley—172 mg.; green pepper—128 mg.; kale—125 mg.; watercress—79 mg.	Kohlrabi, chives, Swiss chard, cabbage, beets, parsnips, carrots, blackberries
Yin				

I.U. = International Units; mg. = milligrams. Values in foods based upon 100 grams of edible portion. Data taken from *Composition and Facts about Foods*, by Ford Heritage.

VITAMIN LOSS IN COOKING

Vitamin	A	B_1	B_2	C	D	E
Cooking Temperature	248° F. 120° C.	248° F. 120° C.	248° F. 120° C.	212° F. 100° C.	248° F. 120° C.	392° F. 170° C.
Cooking Time Before Loss Occurs	several minutes	1 hour	5 hours	20 minutes	4 hours	2 hours
Solubility	oil	water	water	water	oil	oil

Contrary to the belief of many nutritional experts, it can be observed from the chart above that cooking does not destroy vitamins as rapidly as many people assume. However, as shown, vitamins B_1, B_2, and C are all water-soluble, and when preparing foods rich in these vitamins, it is important to avoid prolonged soaking in order to retain as much as possible of the valuable nutrients.

VITAMINS, MINERALS, PROTEINS, ETC. 49

Minerals are interrelated with vitamins: the presence of vitamin D aids in the absorption of calcium and phosphorus; the presence of ascorbic acid aids iron in metabolic functions.

Minerals found naturally in foods are more easily absorbed than when taken in the form of concentrated extractions or supplements. Seaweed is one of the richest sources of most of our required minerals and is also considered an important part of the macrobiotic diet. (See chart on seaweeds in Sea Vegetables section, p. 123.)

The chart on the next page will give some idea of the best sources of minerals.

Protein

Grains, beans, and nuts all contain essential amino acids and so do many leafy green and root vegetables and some fruits. In soybeans alone, the amounts of some essential amino acids are actually higher than the concentrations found in meat. Meat is also a very poor source of all other food elements, minerals, vitamins, and carbohydrates.

A person who depends solely upon animal products for protein may still not be getting as much essential protein from his food as a vegetarian (see chart on p. 52). In addition, he runs the risk of having to burden his digestive system with incomplete proteins. Many proteins from animal foods remain in the stomach too long and permit an overdevelopment of harmful bacteria. The poisons from the bacteria and incompletely digested proteins are worse than waste material because they cannot be assimilated and nature can only get rid of them through the mucous membranes in the form of mucus. If all proteins go through the normal steps of digestion the excess amino acids can be eliminated in urea, uric acid and uratinim in the urine without difficulty.

By maintaining a diet composed of cereal foods with small amounts of other vegetables, we can still enjoy occasional animal food, but do not have to be dependent upon it for sustaining life.

A diet composed largely of good-quality vegetable foods offers large amounts of necessary proteins; in some instances these concentrations are far greater in vegetable foods than in animal products.

Below is a chart comparing the fat and protein content of a small sampling of common foods. Some of the data may surprise you!

MINERALS FOUND IN FOOD WE EAT*

Mineral	Recommended Amount for Adults	Food Source	Function in the Body
Sodium	0.5 grams	Dulse—2,085 mg.;† green leafy vegetables (Swiss chard—147 mg.); dried fruit	Aids in formation of digestive juices, elimination of sulfur dioxide, maintains water balance
Magnesium	30 mg.	Dulse—220 mg.; dried beans–soybeans—265 mg.; lentils—80 mg. and leafy greens; dried fruit	Strengthens nerves and muscles, activates enzymes in carbohydrate metabolism; conditions liver and glands
Iron	10–12 mg.	Dulse—150 mg.; sesame seeds—10.5 mg.; green vegetables–dandelion greens—3.1 mg.; beans, rice	For hemoglobin, bones, brain and muscle tissue formation; oxidative enzymes
Iodine	0.15–30 mg.	Kelp—150 mg.; dulse—8 mg.; Swiss chard—0.099 mg.; watermelon—0.040 mg.; green vegetables	Aids in the oxidation of fats, proteins; stimulates circulation
Potassium	3 grams	Dulse—8,060 mg.; soybeans—1,677 mg.; dried fruit, nuts, vegetables	Aids in elimination, formation of glycogen from glucose, fats from glycogen, regulates heartbeat
Calcium	0.8 grams	Sesame seeds—1,160 mg.; green vegetables; kale—249 mg.; sunflower seeds—120 mg.	Blood coagulation; builds bones, teeth, activates some enzymes; normalizes metabolism
Phosphorus	1.2 grams	Sunflower seeds—837 mg.; nuts, beans; lentils—377 mg.; cereal grains, seaweed, dried fruit	Same as above; transport of fatty acids

* Data compiled from *Composition and Facts about Foods*, by Ford Heritage, and from the *Composition of Foods*, U. S. Agricultural Handbook No. 8.
† Values based upon 100 grams of edible portion of food.

Food Source	Protein	Fat*
Beef	19.3	10.5
Bacon	14.0	37.4
Fish	14.6	0.7
Chicken	17.0	6.7
Soybeans	40.8	23.5
Lentils	23.8	trace
Peanuts	28.1	49.0
Eggs	11.9	12.3
Almonds	20.5	53.5

The amounts of unsaturated fatty acids in vegetable foods are considerably lower than the amount of fat in animal foods.

Soybeans are eaten mainly in the form of miso, soy sauce, and occasionally tofu (soybean curd) in the macrobiotic diet.

* Material presented here is from "Vegetarism" a paper put out by the Vegetarian Society (UK.) Ltd., Parkdale, Dunham Road, Altrincham, Cheshire, England.

CHART ON THE ESSENTIAL AMINO ACIDS BASED ON GRAM PER GRAM OF NITROGEN

Food	Arginine	Cystine	Histidine	Isoleucine	Leucine	Lysine	Methionine	Phenyl-alanine	Threonine	Tryptophane	Tryosine	Valine
Meat Products	0.41	0.08	0.20	0.32	0.49	0.51	0.15	0.26	0.28	0.08	0.21	0.33
Milk and Cheese	0.23	0.05	0.17	0.39	0.62	0.49	0.15	0.32	0.29	0.09	0.35	0.44
Soybeans	0.46	0.12	0.16	0.33	0.48	0.40	0.08	0.31	0.25	0.09	0.23	0.33
Whole Wheat Flour	0.27	0.13	0.13	0.24	0.40	0.17	0.10	0.29	0.18	0.08	0.20	0.27

Fats and Oils

Since we use pure, unrefined vegetable oils in macrobiotic cooking the amount of saturated fats in our diet is very low. In addition, many foods contain good quality vegetable fat, with small percentages of saturated fatty acids. The daily recommended maximum amount of oil in a macrobiotic diet is two tablespoons; this amount finds its way into food through sautéed or fried vegetables, and in sauces, dressings, and spreads made of sesame butter. Small amounts of fat are found in almost all vegetables; oats have the highest amount of fat of all the cereal grains.

Carbohydrates

The macrobiotic diet is rich in carbohydrates. Since digestion of these foods begins in the mouth, chewing is very important. The more we chew our grains, especially brown rice, the sweeter they become. Natural sugars are found in all our foods. There is no need to depend upon concentrated incomplete sugars in the form of refined white sugar, molasses, maple syrup, or honey; these foods merely overtax our digestive system and are virtually empty foods because they offer no food value.

Just Because It's Edible...

JUST BECAUSE a food is edible doesn't mean it's fit for human consumption. A large and still growing number of items that comprise modern man's diet simply no longer fit into the orthodox classification of foods. These "non-foods" offer almost no nutritional value and many of them are harmful as well. Below is a listing of those foods that are virtually excluded from a macrobiotic diet, with the reasons why.

Coffee—Besides being a plant from a tropical climate, and therefore out of balance with our environment in North America, coffee produces a great deal of acid in the body, and high amounts of caffeine act as a stimulant.* Coffee has no food value. If you enjoy the taste of coffee, natural food stores carry a variety of delicious grain coffees that are caffeine-free.

Drugs—All drugs, psychedelic and medical—including marijuana, LSD, aspirin, birth control pills, etc.—are a thousand times more yin than sugar, and their use, if you are following a macrobiotic diet, is not recommended. The psychedelic drugs, whether organic or not, cause serious body malfunctions.

Dyed teas—Almost all commercially harvested teas are dyed. Since many of these dyes are possibly carcinogenic, such teas should be avoided. The alternative is simple—natural green teas, herb teas, teas made from grain or roots, or leaves; they offer many beneficial qualities besides having a naturally sweet taste.

* See *Body, Mind and Sugar*, by E. M. Abrahamson, M.D., and A. W. Pezet, New York: Henry Holt and Company, 1948.

JUST BECAUSE IT'S EDIBLE 55

Canned and processed foods—Almost all commercially prepared foods contain preservatives and additives, not to mention artificial coloring, artificial flavorings, chemical fillers, etc. Most sugar-coated breakfast foods are created in scientific laboratories by chemists; even synthetically enriched or fortified foods cannot successfully replace fresh foods, for the body cannot always absorb the chemical substitutes which were designed to imitate nature.

Chocolate—A tropical bean plant, chocolate not only contains an acid that leaches out calcium from the digestive tract but also contains a substance similar to caffeine. Chocolate is by nature a bitter food, and modern preparations generally contain large amounts of sugar, artificial coloring, and preservatives.

Dairy products—While some animal foods (fish, occasionally eggs or fowl) are included in the macrobiotic diet, dairy products are almost completely eliminated. The cow's milk available today has been altered by pasteurization which destroys natural enzymes, leaving a poor quality food. All the other nutrients found in milk can be obtained in much higher proportion in foods such as seaweeds (which contain 2½ to 14 times as much calcium) and leafy green vegetables. Milk by-products—butter, yogurt, cheeses and cream—contain saturated fats as well as dyes, artificial coloring and preservatives which interfere with digestion.

If you are strongly attracted to dairy products, goat's milk (or raw cow's milk from a government-inspected source) is preferred to regular supermarket milk because it is more digestible and a better source of food. Pure goat products are carried in natural and health food stores.

Eggs—Doctors are beginning to realize the harmful effects of eating too many eggs. Eggs cause putrefaction in the intestines because of the high sulfur content; their high cholesterol content is another good reason to eat them only occasionally.

If you are strongly attracted to eggs, at least obtain them, preferably fertilized, through places that sell eggs that come from organically raised hens. Supermarket eggs come from chicken farm factories where the hens have been sitting in coops all their lives, stuffed with chemicals and subjected to the most unnatural conditions; organic hens are allowed to use their legs and run around the barnyard.

The difference between an organic egg and a chemical one is easy to observe: gently crack the shells of both eggs and drop eggs onto a plate. The organic egg will have a darker clear yolk, with the white forming a definite circle around it—the supermarket egg generally has a pale yolk and a thin runny white.

Frozen food—Freezing has a detrimental effect on the cellular structure of all living things; it causes rapid deterioration when foods are thawed. As the quality of the food is altered important nutrients are lost.

Leavening agents—Baking soda, baking powder, and yeast produce rapid reactions in bread doughs, creating a breakdown in the chemical structure of the food and a quick release of energy. Leavened bread stimulates the production of gastric acid during digestion which shortens the time food remains in the stomach. Unleavened bread can be left to rise naturally overnight, allowing for natural fermentation to take place. This slower method produces a bread that is heavier but more chewy and delicious, and less taxing on the digestive juices.

Meat—Most meats today are filled with chemicals—residues from antibiotics, hormones, and tranquilizers that were shot into or fed to cattle, dyes added by man, and pesticides from foodstuffs consumed by the cattle. Processed meats contain numerous other non-foods, e.g., stabilizers, preservatives, fillers, and artificial flavorings.

Meat takes a long time to digest; it requires tremendous effort on the part of the digestive and circulatory systems to get rid of the toxins and poisons we consume when we eat flesh.* Macrobiotics agrees with vegetarianism that all essential nutrients can be obtained from the vegetable kingdom—including amino acids, fats, carbohydrates, starches, vitamins, and minerals.

Refined oil, margarine and hydrogenated oils—Oil is very important in our cooking. When we eliminate saturated animal fats from our diet and replace them with quality vegetable oils, we must be careful in selecting oils that will supply us with nutrients and unsaturated fatty acids. All hydrogenated oils should be avoided since these are heavily altered, chemically treated products. The best quality oils of vegetable origin are available only through natural food stores. The biggest difference between the quality of vegetable oils found in macrobiotic kitchens and the type the average consumer purchases can be judged just by the senses alone. The oils we use are unrefined, deep in color, and smell exactly like the

---

* See *Nutrition for Health*, by Dr. Alice Chase, Englewood, N.J.: Prentice-Hall, 1967.

plants they come from. They are full of impurities. But these "impurities" are actually nutrients—vitamins A, E, F, and elements like natural lecithin. The other oils appear clear and light—"pure" because they have been highly refined, filtered, deodorized and of course doctored with preservatives to insure their shelf life.

High quality oils carried by natural food stores (and produced by such companies as Erewhon Trading Co. and Walnut Acres Farms—see p. 208) are first expelled, then pressed, using a low heat process; the oils are then clarified by allowing them to sit in settling tanks; then the oil is drawn off through filters and bottled. This is the process that results in a natural unrefined vegetable oil.

Even the light, almost transparent oils carried in health food stores and labeled "cold pressed" look that way because they have been heavily refined with harsh caustic chemicals, heated to high temperatures to remove odor, and finally bottled. They were pressed originally—but the whole story is not described on the label.

The majority of all other oils sold in stores across the country today are prepared by the following means: oil-bearing materials are ground, steam-cooked, and mixed with a solvent (with a petroleum base) that dissolves out the oils. The solvent is then separated from the oil but trace amounts of the solvent still remain. The solvents most commonly used today are light petroleum fractions—some of which are commonly used in gasoline. By the time the oil is bottled practically everything of value has been leached out.

Just about the only pure oil found in a supermarket is imported (virgin) olive oil. It's expensive compared to the other types, but then so are the natural oils carried by macrobiotic food sources. However the price is only relative. Since the amount of oil used in this method of cooking is generally very little (and you are not spending a lot of money on meat), the cost is quite reasonable.

There are several excellent varieties of oil to choose from. Erewhon Trading Co. markets corn germ, sesame, soya, and sunflower oils. All are excellent for use in cooking and contain absolutely no preservatives; furthermore, they are considerably less likely to turn rancid than refined oils because the natural preservative properties have not been removed through bleaching or high temperatures. For further information, see Oil, *The Encyclopedia Britannica*, vol. 16; "Rancidity in Oils," and "The Lowdown on Edible Oils," published by the Lee Foundation for Nutritional Research,

Milwaukee, Wis. Also "The Oil Story," a reprint available through the Organic Merchants, c/o Erewhon Trading Co., 33 Farnsworth St., Boston, Mass. 02210.

Soft drinks and diet colas—While the exact formulas of Coca-Cola and Dr. Pepper remain a secret to the world, it can easily be established through chemical analysis that colas contain caffeine, tannic acid, theobromine, glucose, and sugar, as well as substantial amounts of phosphoric acid and artificial flavoring agents. If you've ever spilled a soft drink on fabric or furniture you are aware of the damage it can do if left untreated—imagine what it does to the walls of your stomach!

Spices—Spices were originally used in hot countries as preservatives. The majority of spices found in supermarkets today are of tropical origin and totally unnecessary for our well-being; with refrigeration and other devices for storing foodstuffs, the need for heavy spicing to preserve or mask unpleasant odors has been eliminated.

Spices stimulate the walls of the stomach and intestines and are often the first thing physicians restrict or eliminate in the diets of people with internal ailments (i.e., ulcers). However, certain herbs and spices—bay leaves, garlic, ginger, oregano, parsley, thyme, and cinnamon—*can* be used in moderation for pleasing effects in cooking.

Chemical flavoring agents and seasonings are to be avoided—they are mineral extracts and totally unnecessary nonfoods.

Sugar, molasses, corn syrup and honey—Cane sugar is not a whole food, merely an extraction from a plant. Since it is illegal in America to sell unrefined sugar, it is heavily processed. During the "refining" treatment, lime, phosphoric acid, and diatomaceous earth all come in contact with the cane. The end product is pure—to the extent that everything possible has been removed. All forms of nonwhite sugars (i.e., raw, brown sugar, and Kleenraw) are made from a white sugar base. After the refining process, molasses is added to white sugar to make "light brown" or "dark brown" sugar; for Kleenraw, a special crystallization process is used to create the illusion of rawness. Molasses, too, is not a whole food, but a by-product produced through chemical treatment of the sugarcane.

Corn syrup is produced by treating cornstarch with sulfuric acid; the resulting product is then neutralized with sodium carbonate and filtered through charred beef bones to produce clarity.

Honey and maple syrup are certainly more "natural products" than cane sugar, but they are not considered good food for man by macrobiotics. Maple sap is just slightly sweet when it comes dripping out of the tree—but it takes fifty gallons of sap to make just one gallon of syrup. There is a mighty big difference between the natural sap and the final concentrated syrup man manufactures. Honey is basically an animal product. The flower nectar undergoes chemical changes in the bee's body—again producing a highly concentrated sugar. With all the natural sugars found in whole foods—in fruits, nuts, vegetables, and grains, additional sugars are unnecessary and can produce numerous physical ailments. If you are dependent on sweetening agents, at least try to switch to honey or maple syrup, and slowly reduce your intake until you are no longer dependent upon sugar.

Tap water—Everyone is aware that our natural resources have suffered through man's carelessness. Water is just one of many essential foods that man has affected and misused to such an extent that good water is becoming scarce.

Spring water is preferred over tap water in cooking. It is usually not treated with chemicals and has a cleaner taste. However, there are no government regulations regarding the bottling of spring water to date, and the market is somewhat open right now to many questionable suppliers.

Tap water is certainly loaded with undesirable trace compounds, minerals, and chemicals. If you find it difficult to get good spring water or well water in your vicinity, the next best thing is to boil water from the tap for at least five minutes before using it for cooking. Inexpensive and highly effective carbon filters are also recommended—these may be purchased through natural food stores for about eleven dollars. We have been using ours for a long time—it's portable and we always take it with us on trips.

Treating water may sound like an extreme and unnecessary burden, but the difference in your health can quickly be observed in a few days. The hard compounds in water place an extra burden on the kidneys which have the job of filtering them out, and often mineral deposits simply collect in various organs. Also the trace chemicals in water have a definite effect on food—bread made with tap water cannot rise naturally because the chemicals in the water actually inhibit or kill the natural yeasting agents.

Once you become accustomed to the taste of filtered, spring, or well water, you'll be reluctant to drink straight tap water again.

Grains

IT HAS BEEN NOTED by scientists that food emanates subtle vibratory forces. These forces, called "life energy factors," have been detected with special sensitive instruments. Through these, it has been determined that whole grain is much more alive than grain that has been milled. Grain is both the seed and the fruit of the grass plant. It contains all the essential elements needed for a new cycle of life. That is one of the reasons why the macrobiotic diet recommends more grains than other vegetable foods. It is best to eat them in a whole state, just as they are found in nature.

Cracked grain or flaked grain is not as full of life energy, for the germ of each kernel has been shattered. Milling grain into flour further reduces this vital force. Unless you have a flour mill and can grind your own flour immediately before use, it is better to avoid using incomplete grain as much as possible. Flour and slightly processed grains are handy to have around for occasional use, but we try not to become dependent upon them as regular foods.

Since grains are considered the primary food of a macrobiotic diet, it is important to learn how to cook them properly and to find out which varieties are best suited for your climate and individual needs. Rice is the most superior grain from a nutritional standpoint and composes the main part of our diet, but the other grains offer a pleasing change and help to accent and complement rice. If you are not familiar with these other grains, a whole new world is yours to discover and explore.

Brown Rice

A friend of mine, a free-lance photographer, once invited me to his studio to see some color slides of the people in Asia, a record of his recent trip to the Orient. I eagerly accepted his offer as I had been eating brown rice for three months and was very curious about the eating habits of people who had depended upon rice for thousands of years.

The slides were wonderfully vivid; many of them showed the marketplaces of Pakistan, Thailand, and Ceylon, where the vegetables and fruits glowed like jewels in the intense sunlight against a background of whitewashed buildings, dark-eyed women shrouded in veils, and gaunt, wrinkled merchants. Ripe mangoes, oranges, tomatoes, eggplants, and beans overflowed from their baskets. Suspended from wooden beams were slaughtered fowl and cooked meats. Here and there was an occasional sack of grain or white rice.

"Where is the brown rice?" I asked my friend.

"Brown rice?" He laughed. "I've been in markets all over Asia and never once saw brown rice. White rice—in the restaurants, the shops, the open kitchens—is the only rice sold."

"Are you sure?"

"I never saw brown rice," he said, smiling.

It took several years for me to accept this truth. Milled rice, polished rice, was once only for the rich. With industrialization came more mills, and now millions of people, almost half the world's population, eat white rice exclusively—simply because brown rice traditionally has been associated with poverty. If you go to eating places in Japan and ask for brown rice you may be laughed at.

Cooked brown rice contains 25 percent more protein than white rice, and is higher in calcium, iron, phosphorus, thiamine, riboflavin, and niacin.

Brown rice is low in cholesterol, contains only a trace of

fat, and is practically free of saturated fats.* It is gluten-free and very easy to digest because of a low fiber content, which thereby makes it a non-allergy food. Rice is a good principal food, and not only from a statistical point of view—it also tastes good!

Many diets come close to macrobiotics but do not place as much emphasis on grain. The true macrobiotic diet tries to maintain a minimum of 50 percent grain, and the most versatile, wholesome grain happens to be brown rice.

There are endless ways of preparing rice. However, rice is always lighter when made with only a minimum amount of salt, just a pinch for each cup of uncooked grain. The most important thing to remember when eating rice is the chewing. The more you chew, the sweeter it becomes. Chewing is important because it is a part of our digestion process, and in order to get the most from our food, we must chew it thoroughly.

Just cooking rice can teach you many things. You will be able to tell when the rice is done by smell, not by a clock. On some days you may prefer rice that is cooked with less pressure and steamed or boiled. The quality of the grain you are using also makes a big difference. The short-grain brown rice is more yang, the longer varieties more yin. You may want to try other varieties for a change, but short-grain brown rice is the rice of the everyday diet.

Look for grains that are uniform in size and shape and not discolored or chipped. Always wash the rice carefully in cold water several times before cooking. Use a strainer to drain off excess water between rinsings. It is easiest to wash the rice right in the pot; this way hulls and any dirt will float to the top and can be removed without any trouble. Use your hand to wash the rice, swirling it around in a counter-clockwise direction. This natural centripetal movement complies with the yang force of the earth.

Boiled Rice—Basic Preparation

2 to 3 servings

1 cup short-grain brown rice   ⅛ teaspoon salt
2 cups water

Wash the rice carefully several times in cold water. Place

---

* Solid, or saturated, fats are conducive to a high level of cholesterol when taken to excess. Foods containing saturated fats are hydrogenated cooking fats, margarines, processed cheeses, nondairy creamers, and hydrogenated peanut butter. All natural oils found in vegetable quality food are high in unsaturated fats.

the rice in a heavy saucepan; add *cold* water and bring to a boil. Add the salt and cover the pot with a tight-fitting lid. Place an asbestos pad underneath the pan and reduce the flame. Simmer over a low heat for at least 50 minutes.

After turning off the flame, let rice sit for 10 minutes to steam. Mix gently with a rice paddle or wooden spoon before serving. The rice should be lightly scorched to a yellowish color on the bottom. This part is very yang; it contains minerals that settled out during cooking and should never be discarded.

Boiled rice is a more yin preparation than pressure-cooked, but it is nice to have once in a while and is especially good in summer or for breakfast. If you cannot obtain a pressure cooker, roast the rice slightly in a dry skillet for about 10 minutes, or until it begins to pop, which will make it a little more chewy. If you are not using short-grain brown rice, you may find it necessary to add a little more water. Also, in summer, for softer rice, more liquid can be used.

VARIATIONS: Try boiling rice in bancha tea instead of water, or add 1 tablespoon of sesame seeds, or 1 salted plum for each cup of raw rice, or 1 tablespoon of tamari in place of the salt.

Pressure-Cooked Rice

2 servings

1 cup short-grain brown rice ⅛ teaspoon salt
1¼ to 1½ cups water

Wash rice carefully several times in cold water. It is easiest to wash it directly in the pot, and drain off excess water through a fine mesh strainer. Add the cooking water and salt, and cover. Bring to full pressure over a high flame. When regulator begins to jiggle, reduce flame and slide an asbestos pad under the pot and cook for another 40 to 50 minutes.

Let pressure drop to normal before removing lid. Mix gently with a rice paddle and serve.

The larger the amount of rice you are preparing, the less water will be needed. If you are making more than 2 or 3 cups of raw rice at a time, the water can be reduced about ⅛ of a cup per cup of rice. During the summer, for fluffy rice, you can remove the regulator about 5 minutes after turning off the flame and let the steam escape through the valve for another 5 minutes before removing the lid.

Baked Rice

5 to 6 servings

2 cups brown rice
⅛ teaspoon salt *or* 1 tablespoon tamari

3½ to 4 cups boiling water

After washing the rice, dry-roast it in a hot skillet over a medium flame until the rice begins to pop. Place in a Pyrex or earthenware casserole dish and add salt or tamari. Add boiling water and cover. Baked in a preheated 375° oven for 50 to 60 minutes.

Rice or Whole-Grain Porridge

4 servings

1 cup brown rice
5 cups water

pinch of salt

Bring washed rice to a boil, lower flame and add salt; cover and place over an asbestos pad; simmer for 1½ to 2 hours.

For special rice cream, first dry-roast rice and after cooking purée in a Foley food mill. Leftover bran may be saved for breads, muffins, etc.

When using other grains, for a sweeter taste, always dry-roast for 10 minutes before cooking. For variation, add thinly sliced sautéed vegetables, or roasted nuts or seeds, to the porridge. Cooked porridge is also good garnished with chopped scallions or parsley or served with toasted nori or wakame seaweed and tamari.

Rice Cream Made from Prepared Powder

4 servings

1 cup rice cream powder
½ teaspoon sesame oil (optional)

4 cups water
⅛ teaspoon salt

If desired, sauté the powder in ½ teaspoon of sesame oil to sweeten it. Otherwise dry-roast in a heavy saucepan for a few minutes until there is a nutlike fragrance. Let the powder cool slightly before slowly adding water. Bring to a boil, add salt, and cover. Let simmer over an asbestos pad for 30 to 40 minutes, stirring occasionally to prevent scorching.

For pressure cooking, reduce cooking time to 20 minutes.

Fried Rice
2 servings

2 teaspoons oil
2 cups cooked rice
1 tablespoon tamari

Heat oil in a skillet. Add rice and gently break up grain with a rice paddle or chopsticks. Continue to stir, turning grains over constantly for 10 minutes. Sprinkle with tamari and cook a few more minutes.

Fried Rice with Vegetables
4 servings

2 tablespoons oil
4 scallions, chopped
¼ cup cooked seaweed *or* several sheets of nori*
¼ cup slivered root vegetables (carrots, burdock, etc.)
4 cups cooked rice
2 tablespoons tamari

Heat oil in a skillet and add scallions. Sauté for a few minutes before adding seaweed and root vegetables. Add rice and continue to sauté, gently tossing vegetables and grain with a rice paddle or cooking chopsticks for another 5 minutes. Add tamari and stir once lightly. Cover pan and let steam a few minutes before serving.

Sushi

Sushi is the Japanese term for rice and chopped or grated vegetables, rolled in sheets of nori or wakame seaweed, and then cut into small rounds. It is a decorative finger food that makes attractive hors d'oeuvres for a buffet or picnic and is a delightful addition to a summer lunch.

For each roll, use:

1½ cups soft rice (rice prepared with 2½ parts water if pressure-cooked, 3 parts if boiled)
¼ cup grated carrot
2 tablespoons minced watercress or scallion, *or* 1 tablespoon chives
1 sheet toasted nori or wakame (see recipe for Fried Rice for directions on toasting)
sushi mat or bamboo placemat†

---

* If using nori, pass a sheet back and forth over an open flame for a few seconds until the seaweed becomes crisp and changes color. Crumple sheet with your hands over the skillet.

† Available in Oriental and specialty kitchenware shops.

66 GRAINS

Place a sheet of toasted seaweed on the sushi mat. Pat rice on one half of the sheet and arrange vegetables in a horizontal row down the center of the rice.

Wet your fingers with a little water to prevent the seaweed from sticking to your fingers, and starting at the side with the rice, roll the sheet toward the other end. Use the sushi mat to keep the roll a uniform shape. Roll should be about 1½ inches in diameter.

Place roll on a cutting board or plate, and using a sharp knife, cut into circles about 1 inch thick. Arrange on a platter.

VARIATIONS: Use chopped nuts and raisins or apples for sweet sushi. Sushi may be garnished with a sprinkle of sesame salt or minced parsley.

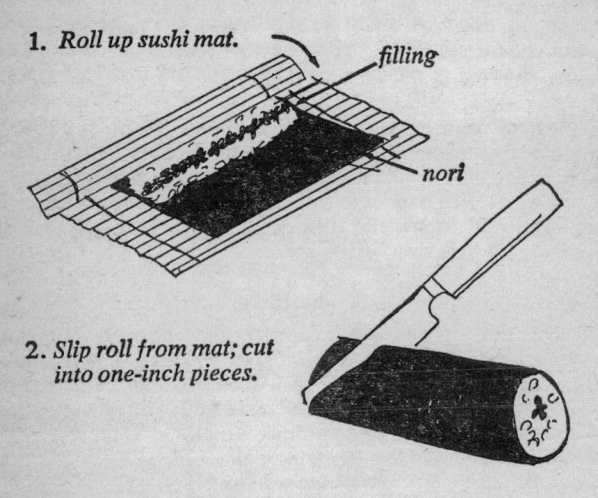

1. Roll up sushi mat.

filling

nori

2. Slip roll from mat; cut into one-inch pieces.

3. Serve on a platter.

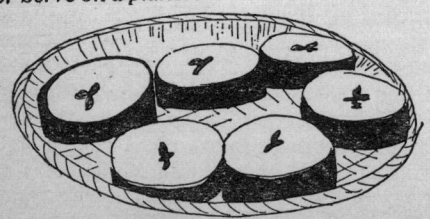

Sweet Brown Rice

Sweet brown rice is a very short, plump variety of rice high in glutinous content and therefore excellent for making breads and desserts. It is also used in making sweet rice wine. It has a much more sticky consistency than regular brown rice. The Japanese use sweet rice and aduki beans together for a traditional holiday dish; the beans and rice are first soaked together overnight in about two or three times as much water and then cooked the next day in the same way rice alone is usually prepared. If you want to make aduki sweet rice, try using 1 part beans to 4 parts rice, and vary the proportions afterward to suit your taste.

Mochi is to the Japanese what bread is to us. Traditional Japanese mochi is made several ways. One method uses steamed sweet rice that is pounded with an equal amount of flour, steamed again, and finally baked or fried. The whole process takes over 2 hours, but is well worth the effort. However, since most of us can't take that much time to prepare mochi, here is a short-cut flourless method that uses aduki beans.

Aduki Mochi

Makes 3 dozen mochi

2 cups sweet brown rice (you can use regular brown rice here if sweet rice is hard to find)	½ cup aduki beans ½ teaspoon salt ¼ cup sesame seeds oil

Pressure-cook the rice and beans together in 4½ cups water, bringing the pot up to pressure with a medium flame. Cook for only 30 minutes once full pressure is reached; let pot sit undisturbed for another ½ hour.

For regular cooking, boil the aduki beans for 30 minutes in a covered pan using 1½ cups water; remove from heat, add rice and 3½ cups water, and bring to a boil again. Cover pan, reduce flame, and let simmer for 40 minutes. Turn off heat and let sit undisturbed another 20 minutes to steam.

While the rice is still hot, remove about half the mixture and transfer to a suribachi or food mill. Purée the rice until it becomes quite soft, and add to the whole rice. Add salt. Using a wet rice paddle or wet hands, knead the batter to blend rice. If rice is too sticky to work with, keep dipping your hands in cold water.

Shape into patties ½ inch thick and 3 inches in diameter. Sprinkle each with sesame seeds.

Either fry until lightly browned in a skillet brushed with oil, or bake on an oiled cookie sheet for 20 minutes in a 375° oven. If baking, turn mochi cakes after 10 minutes for uniform cooking. Mochi may also be deep-fried if rolled into smaller balls.

Any leftovers should be refrigerated, as the beans ferment rather quickly. Uncooked patties should be refrigerated until ready to fry or bake, and will keep fresh in the refrigerator for several days.

Mochi is good in soups as a soft dumpling. Chopped nuts, raisins, grated apples, or chestnuts make tasty additions for dessert mochi. These may be cooked with the rice and beans, or added just before the baking. If you are using dried chestnuts, be sure to soak them first and either pressure-cook or boil them before adding to the batter.

Barley

Barley is a small white kernel with a fine brownish line running down the center separating each grain into two tiny chambers. A barley grain is even smaller than a grain of short brown rice, and its digestability has long been recognized by physicians who recommend it as a baby food. Barley cultivation dates back to prehistoric times, and originated somewhere in Syria and northern Egypt. Cooked alone as a grain, it can be made into a light, chewy breakfast cereal, or, with less water, it makes a chewy dish similar to rice in texture. Barley teams up splendidly with all types of lentils and can also be combined with other cooked grains for variety.

It is a good source of vitamins and minerals and is excellent to use in summer because of its lightness. Barley flour is fine and sweet and especially good in cookie, pastry, and bread doughs. For additional recipes using barley, see index.

Barley Porridge

4 servings

1 cup barley, washed   ¼ teaspoon salt
4 to 5 cups water

Dry-roast barley first in a cast-iron skillet over a high flame until lightly browned. Place the roasted grain in a heavy saucepan with the water and salt. Bring to a boil, then lower flame and cover. Slip an asbestos pad under the pan and let simmer for 1½ hours.

Note: *Barley porridge should not be pressure-cooked;** the starch released during cooking will clog up the safety valve, causing excess liquid to flow out of regulator.

Leftover porridge makes wonderful puddings or can be added to soups or breads.

Barley with Vegetables
6 servings

1 tablespoon oil	2 cups barley, washed and dry-roasted
1 onion, cut into slivers	¼ teaspoon sea salt
2 to 3 carrots, cut into small pieces	4 cups water
½ cup chopped watercress (or other leafy green vegetable)	

Sauté the vegetables in oil for about 10 minutes in the order given, allowing a few minutes between each addition. Add the roasted barley and continue to sauté for another few minutes.

If using a pressure cooker, the sautéing may be done directly in the cooker. Add 4 cups of water and salt, and cover. Bring up to full pressure over a high flame; when full pressure is reached, reduce flame and cook for 40 minutes.

For regular cooking, use a deep skillet and boil the water while the vegetables are sautéing. Pour boiling water over sautéed vegetables and barley. Reduce flame, cover, and let simmer 45 to 50 minutes.

Barley Cakes
Makes 2 dozen cakes

1 cup barley	2 tablespoons oil
1 cup buckwheat flour	½ to ¾ cup water
¼ teaspoon salt	¼ cup roasted sesame seeds

Mix the dry ingredients together in a deep bowl; add the oil and rub it into the flour using fingertips only. Add the

---

* Barley may be pressure-cooked when prepared with other ingredients, including oil and less water. The other ingredients create a coating action that prevents the starch from overflowing.

water slowly, using just enough to hold the dough together. Knead for 10 minutes until it is soft and pliable.

Pinch off small amounts of the dough and roll into balls about 1½ inches in diameter. Flatten the balls with your palms or use a lightly floured glass to spread them to a 3-inch diameter. Then sprinkle each flattened cake with sesame seeds and press again to force seeds into the dough.

Fry on a griddle lightly brushed with oil for 10 minutes, turning several times to insure uniform cooking. Or, if you prefer, bake on a lightly oiled cookie sheet for 15 to 20 minutes.

These cakes are somewhat like crackers and are very good as snacks.

Kasha

My grandmother used to make huge pots of buckwheat every night before going to sleep; that way a filling breakfast was always ready for her four sons and husband. They ate buckwheat out of necessity, not choice, for it was during the Depression and it was the food of the poor people who had brought with them foods from the Old World.

When I was a little girl my father would make kasha from buckwheat groats, and I used to stand on a chair and watch him carefully sauté the groats before pouring over the boiling water to make cereal. Kasha was the only whole "grain" we were familiar with, aside from an occasional pot of long-grain brown rice during the winter as a change from potatoes. Leftover kasha usually found itself in a bowl of soup the next day, or fried with an egg into a crisp, heavy pancake.

When I moved away from home I would often make kasha for breakfast, and flavor it lavishly with milk and honey. Now that I make kasha with a little more understanding, I balance its yang qualities with a green yin vegetable, such as scallions, or serve it with a side dish of sautéed vegetables.

Buckwheat has been the staple food of many regions where the environment is harsh, with long winters, a cold climate, and poor soil. This combination of factors has produced a yang plant that gives as much body heat as meat, and for this reason it should be eaten much less frequently in summer.

Roasted groats are easily ground into flour and make excellent pancakes, but it helps to mix in another flour such as whole wheat or rice, to prevent a heavy batter. Also, when using buckwheat flour in bread, only a small amount is necessary; otherwise the bread will be a leaden disappointment.

Buckwheat Groats (Kasha)

4 servings

1 teaspoon oil
1 cup buckwheat
2 cups boiling water
⅛ teaspoon salt

Heat oil in a skillet and sauté the groats for a few minutes, stirring constantly. If you are using the white unroasted groats, sauté for at least 10 minutes to remove bitterness, or until groats turn a dark nut-brown color.

Add boiling water and salt and cover pan. Lower flame and cook just 15 minutes.

Serve buckwheat with cooked green vegetables or onions because buckwheat is very yang and should be balanced with a more yin vegetable food.

VARIATIONS: Sauté 2 onions in oil and add to buckwheat while it is being sautéed. A pinch of thyme can be added for a change of taste. Try using 3 to 4 cups of water if serving it as a breakfast food.

Buckwheat Cream

3 to 4 servings

¼ cup oil
¼ cup buckwheat flour
2 cups water
dash of salt

Heat oil in a saucepan and add flour; sauté for a few minutes, add water, and cook over a low heat, stirring constantly until thick. This may be served as a breakfast dish, or flavored with tamari and chopped scallions and used as a sauce over grain or noodles.

Kasha Croquettes

Makes 1 dozen croquettes

2 cups cooked buckwheat groats
1 onion, minced
1 tablespoon minced parsley
1 tablespoon tamari
¾ cup cooked rice
corn oil

Mix all ingredients except the rice and oil in a bowl. Pound the rice in a suribachi until it becomes almost pastelike. Mix with the other ingredients, using a wet rice paddle or your fingers (but keep a small bowl of water nearby so you can wet them frequently to prevent the dough from sticking).

Wet fingers and shape dough into small balls about 1 inch in diameter. These may be sautéed in a small amount of oil, or deep-fried in a larger amount of oil, or flattened out and placed on an oiled cookie sheet and baked for 15 minutes in a 375° oven.

VARIATIONS: Use ½ cup whole wheat or corn flour and ¼ cup water in place of the rice. Serve croquettes with noodles, or in soup, or use to garnish a salad.

Kasha Spoon Bread
Serves 6 to 8

1 cup corn flour
2 cups boiling water
1 cup sautéed vegetables
2½ cups cooked kasha
2 tablespoons corn oil or sunflower oil
⅛ teaspoon sea salt

Roast the corn flour in a dry skillet for several minutes until it begins to turn a deeper color. Pour flour into a deep mixing bowl and scald with the boiling water. Mix in the remaining ingredients, reserving a small amount of the oil for greasing a casserole dish.

Pour the mixture into the baking dish and bake 40 to 50 minutes in a 350° oven.

For variety, try a combination of other cooked grains or flour with the kasha. Sweet rice, barley, or oat flour may be used in place of the corn. This bread is delicious when served with a light sauce, such as béchamel (see p. 158), and even better the next day when thinly sliced and pan-fried or lightly toasted.

Corn

There are many distinctly different varieties of corn existing today. Most of them are highly developed hybrids, quite different from the tiny husks of wild corn found by the natives of South America thousands of years ago. Fresh corn is a delicious vegetable and needs very little cooking. However, the corn developed for use as a grain is quite different. The variety of large kernels we use for cornmeal or corn flour is not quite suitable for cooking the way we would prepare another grain, such as barley or oats. Even if it is soaked for several days and pressure-cooked for a few hours it remains quite fibrous and starchy.

If you have a grain mill and want to make meal, first rinse the kernels briefly in cold water to remove any foreign matter. Dry-roast them in a dry cast-iron skillet until they become parched and start to crack. They will be much easier to grind if prepared this way. If you don't own a mill, purchase only small quantities of cornmeal at a time since it spoils quickly. A light roasting helps freshen stored flour.

White cornmeal is slightly sweeter than the yellow variety and is good in puddings and cakes. The yellow cornmeal is excellent in breads and for cereal; these varieties can be used interchangeably.

Cornmeal for Breakfast

4 servings

1 cup cornmeal	4 cups water
½ teaspoon oil	¼ teaspoon salt

Sauté the cornmeal in a heavy saucepan with the oil. Stir constantly to prevent burning. When the cornmeal develops a fragrance and is lightly browned, remove from heat. Let cool slightly before slowly adding water. Bring back to stove and let cereal come to a boil.

Reduce flame, add a pinch of salt, cover, and let simmer 30 to 40 minutes over an asbestos pad to prevent burning.

Leftover corn cereal can be fried in a little corn oil and served with a dash of tamari. It also makes great fritters when mixed with some whole grain such as rice, or fresh corn kernels, flour, and a little chopped green vegetable, and deep-fried. Or it can be made into dumplings and boiled in soup. Try adding leftover cereal to soup as a thickening agent.

Corn Pancakes

Makes 12 large pancakes

1 cup cornmeal	⅓ cup whole wheat, rice, or buckwheat flour
2½ cups boiling water	1 teaspoon sesame oil
¼ teaspoon salt	corn oil for frying

Dry-roast the cornmeal in a skillet until it is lightly toasted. Place in a bowl and cover with scalding water; add salt. Mix briefly with a chopstick to remove lumps.

Mix with other ingredients and pour batter in a hot, oiled skillet.

74 GRAINS

VARIATIONS: Add sesame seeds to the batter, or whole cooked corn kernels. For a sweet pancake, add soybean flour or a little chestnut flour to batter.

Baked Corn on the Cob

whole ears of corn with the husks
tamari or sesame salt

Open ears by gently peeling back the husks and remove the silk. Sprinkle corn with tamari or sesame salt, then replace the husks and bake in a hot 425° oven for 15 minutes. If desired, the corn may be lightly brushed with a small amount of oil before baking.

This is the best way to prepare corn when camping; a wood campfire definitely improves the flavor.

Boiled Corn

whole ears of corn, silk and husks removed
water, just enough to make a 2-inch depth in a kettle
pinch of salt

Bring water to a boil and add corn; when water returns to a boil, add salt, cover, and let steam for 10 minutes. Turn off flame and let corn cook for a few more minutes. Save cooking water for soups or bread.

PRESSURE-COOKED CORN: Place just a small amount of water in cooker (about ½ inch of water is sufficient). Add a pinch of salt, ears of corn, cover, and bring pressure up over a high flame. Reduce flame when pressure comes up, and continue cooking 2 to 3 minutes. Turn off heat and let pressure drop normally.

Oats

Northern Europe has been eating oats since prehistoric times, and today cultivation of this grain is worldwide. Oatmeal makes a hearty winter breakfast, for it has the highest fat content of all grains and is also high in protein. A small amount of miso mixed into cooked oatmeal fortifies it even more.

Although most of us are familiar with oat flakes, whole

oats are simple to prepare and taste even better. The following method for cooking them overnight brings out the flavor and creamy goodness.

Old-Fashioned Oat Porridge
4 servings

1 cup oat groats
5 cups water
⅛ teaspoon salt

Wash the oat groats several times in cold water in a cooking pot. Remove any hulls that float to the top. Drain and dry-roast the groats in a skillet over a high flame, stirring constantly until they are uniformly toasted.

Boil the water, add oats and salt, then reduce flame and cover. Simmer overnight on an asbestos pad with a very low flame.

If you want to cook this more quickly, pressure-cook for 2 hours; remove cover after pressure falls and simmer uncovered until ready to serve.

Oats become extremely sweet when cooked this way and don't require any additional flavoring agents. However, for children or people just getting used to eating grains, the addition of toasted seeds or crushed nuts will make this dish even more appealing.

VARIATIONS: To make a dessert pudding, add ¼ to ½ cup of currants during the cooking and/or a grated apple plus a generous pinch of cinnamon. It's good either warm or cold.

Millet

Millet is the traditional food of the people living in Eurasia. In India alone, there are about six different varieties of this grain. In America millet is most commonly found in commercial birdseed. The millet carried in health and natural foodstores throughout the USA is easily identified by very small, spherical kernels that are light yellow in appearance. Cooked millet is fluffy and white.

Millet makes excellent flour, but as this is sometimes hard to obtain, it is best to grind your own in a handmill. Miller is also very easy to sprout; for directions, see pp. 82–83.

After rinsing millet, dry-roast in a skillet to remove water, then sauté in a small amount of oil (sesame or corn germ). This brings out the natural flavor of the grain and removes

76 GRAINS

any bitterness. Roast until the kernels become a rich golden yellow. Millet can be cooked with sautéed or chopped raw vegetables and tastes even better accompanied by a light sauce.

Millet and Onions
5 servings

1 cup millet	3 cups boiling water
2 onions, sliced and sautéed in 1 teaspoon sesame oil	pinch of salt

Sauté millet until it is golden in a heavy saucepan or skillet, and add the onions. The onions can be sautéed first in the same pan, then set aside for the millet. Add boiling water and salt, and cover. Simmer 30 minutes. For pressure cooking, follow same directions as above, but use cold water. Pressure-cook 25 to 30 minutes. Millet comes out very fluffy if slightly more water is used.

VARIATIONS: Add other cooked vegetables, or chopped parsley, scallion, or watercress. Leftover millet is very good sprinkled with tamari and lightly fried in corn oil.

Millet Casserole
5 servings

Cook millet as directed above, but omit onions. While millet is cooking, sauté ½ cup each carrots and onions, and 1 cup cabbage; all should be cut into thin slivers. In a deep casserole dish, alternate layers of cooked millet with vegetables and pour over a generous amount of béchamel sauce,* sprinkle with crushed nuts, toasted oat flakes, or bread crumbs, and bake in a 350° oven until top is lightly browned.

VARIATIONS: Add cooked chickpeas, aduki beans, or soybeans to casserole.

Millet Croquettes
Makes 18 croquettes

2 cups cooked millet	2 tablespoons tamari
1 onion, finely chopped	½ cup whole wheat flour
¼ cup chopped green vegetables (cabbage, watercress, dandelion greens, etc.)	

* For making sauce, see p. 158.

Mix all ingredients in a bowl and knead with your fingers for 5 to 10 minutes. If dough is hard, add a little water or soup stock. Roll into balls about 1 inch in diameter and deep-fry. Or flatten balls on an oiled cookie sheet and bake in a hot (400°) oven until brown and crisp.

Leftover millet is wonderful in soups and breads, and also tastes good mixed with rice and lightly fried.

Wheat

From the point of view of nutrition and taste wheat is one of the most valuable grains. It has been cultivated for thousands of years and extensive growing has produced a wide variety of different strains. It is lower in fat content, higher in protein, and slightly lower in carbohydrates than rice. Kernels vary in hardness and size according to the area in which they were grown and the planting season. Hard (winter) wheat makes a heavier flour, while spring wheat produces a lighter, finer flour. Most of us eat wheat exclusively in the form of flour in noodles, sauces, or breads, or in a partially processed form, such as bulgar, cracked wheat, couscous, or wheat flakes.

However, whole cooked wheat makes a surprisingly tasty dish. Because it is more fibrous than rice, it is usually prepared with another grain or with beans. Before cooking whole wheat it's best to dry-roast the berries in a skillet for 10 minutes over a medium flame, or else soak the berries overnight, and use the soaking water in cooking.

When pressure-cooking wheat, use about 2 to 3 times as much water as wheat and cook for at least an hour. For regular cooking, 3 to 4 times as much water is necessary. Prepare the same way as for rice, but lengthen cooking time to 1½ or even 2 hours.

Wheat Berries and Rice

5 servings

⅔ cup wheat berries, soaked overnight
1½ cups rice
⅛ teaspoon salt
5 cups water

For regular cooking, place all ingredients in a heavy saucepan and bring to a rolling boil; lower flame and cover, place an asbestos pad under pot, and let simmer 1½ to 2 hours.

78 GRAINS

For pressure cooking, place all ingredients in pot and bring pressure up over a high flame. When regulator begins to spin, lower flame, slip an asbestos pad underneath, and let cook 1 hour.

The rice will be very soft in contrast to the chewy wheat berries. Serve with tamari for breakfast, or mix with sautéed vegetables and bake in a 350° oven for 15 to 20 minutes.

VARIATIONS: Try different proportions of wheat to rice; or use other grains, such as barley or oats.

Wheat Berries and Black Beans

Soak equal amounts of wheat berries and black beans 8 hours, or overnight. Use about 3½ parts water for each part beans and wheat for pressure cooking; increase amount to 4½ parts water for regular cooking.

For pressure cooking, cook 1 hour with pressure. Let pressure drop normally and remove lid. Simmer over a medium flame for another 30 minutes or longer, seasoning with a little salt and tamari. Add a sautéed onion, if desired. For regular cooking, let simmer 2 hours before adding salt or tamari; continue cooking for another 30 to 60 minutes.

Fried Wheat Berries
5 servings

1½ tablespoons oil
6 shallots, minced*
¼ cup chopped watercress or parsley
2 carrots, diced
4 cups cooked wheat berries
¼ cup water or soup stock
2 tablespoons tamari

Heat the oil in a heavy skillet over a medium flame. Sauté vegetables in the order listed, allowing each to cook a minute or two before adding the next one. Continue to sauté for another 5 minutes.

Add the wheat berries and stir gently until the vegetables and wheat are well mixed. Continue to stir for another 3 minutes. Add the liquid and tamari, cover, and let simmer for 5 minutes.

Leftover fried wheat is good in croquettes: mix with a little flour, water, and another grain, and either pan-fry or bake.

---

* Shallots are a small bulb-shaped member of the onion family that bear a strong resemblance to garlic. If you can't get any, try substituting 2 crushed cloves of garlic and 1 medium-sized minced onion.

Wheat Products

BULGAR

Bulgar can be prepared exactly like buckwheat groats. It is most delicious when cooked with sautéed vegetables and makes a satisfying breakfast cereal. Bulgar is also a good filling agent for pastries, breads, cakes, and muffins. It can be prepared with a mild herb or two; a bay leaf or thyme complement its subtle taste.

COUSCOUS

Couscous is more of a specialty food or delicacy than a staple part of the standard macrobiotic diet—it's been processed more than bulgar and also is rather expensive compared to other grains. However, it is delicious when properly prepared and makes a good special-occasion dish as well as light puddings, cakes, or breads. If you don't have an expensive couscous steamer (very few people do), the best and easiest preparation is the boiling method.

Use 1½ parts water for each part couscous. (More water can be used, but it makes a stickier couscous that's suitable for fillings.) Bring water to a boil in a heavy saucepan, add a pinch of salt and couscous. Let it simmer a minute or two. Cover immediately, turn off flame, and let sit for 10 minutes to steam. Serve with a sauce and vegetables.

CRACKED WHEAT

Unless you have a mill, buy only small quantities at a time. Cracked wheat is mainly used as a breakfast cereal, but leftovers have as many uses as bulgar. Toast it for several minutes before cooking to bring out the nutty flavor. For exact cooking directions, see section on cracked cereals.

WHEAT FLAKES

Several excellent brands of macrobiotic wheat flakes have recently been made available. Wheat flakes may be used just like oat flakes; however, it is best to roast them lightly before using. They are great in crunchy toppings, in place of flour in pie crusts, or as a thickening agent. For cooking directions, see pp. 80–81.

Cream Cereals

4 servings

1 cup grain flour (rice, wheat, barley, etc.)
1 teaspoon oil
4 cups liquid (water, soup stock, or tea)
½ teaspoon salt

Roast the flour in oil in a 1½-quart saucepan over a medium flame, stirring constantly to prevent burning. Remove pan from heat and let flour cool slightly before slowly adding the liquid.

Return to stove and cook over a medium flame, stirring occasionally until cream comes to a boil. Add salt, cover and lower flame. Let simmer for another 25 to 30 minutes over an asbestos pad. Stir once or twice during cooking.

To pressure-cook cereal, follow directions for roasting flour, then add cold water, mix thoroughly, and bring pressure up over a high flame. Reduce flame and cook 10 minutes. Let pressure drop normally and serve.

Cream cereals can be used as a base for soups or sauces, or even light dessert creams with the addition of chopped, dried, or cooked fruit, nuts, or sesame butter. If serving a cream cereal as a soup, garnish with chopped scallions or toasted nori seaweed, and flavor with tamari.

Cracked Cereals

If you have a grain mill, you can make your own cereals fresh when you need them. Otherwise, buy only small quantities at a time to ensure freshness.

To begin, wash the grains carefully in cold water several times. Drain in a strainer and dry-roast in a cast-iron skillet until the grain just begins to pop and there is no more steam coming from the pan. Roast only the amount you need. Loosen the grinding stone so that the grain will easily be milled and only slightly cracked. The grain only needs to be milled once.

Preparation of Cracked Rye or Wheat

3 to 4 servings

1 cup cracked grain
3 cups water
pinch of salt

Bring water to a boil in a saucepan, slowly add cereal and salt so that water never stops boiling. Reduce flame, cover, and cook for about 35 to 40 minutes.

For pressure cooking, add cereal and water and salt to pot, bring pressure up over a high flame, reduce flame, and cook for 30 minutes. Remove regulator 5 minutes after turning off heat, let stand another 5 minutes before removing cover.

Leftover cereal is good in breads and muffins and in casseroles.

Flakes of Grain

Besides oat flakes, flakes made from all other grains and buckwheat are now available. These flakes are very good to use in place of flour as a thickening agent in soups and are good for making cookies, pie crusts, and other baked goods, as well as being handy for puddings, casseroles, and desserts. Prepared alone, they are nice for breakfast either boiled or baked.

Boiled Flakes
3 to 4 servings

1 cup oat, millet, or rye flakes (or mix them for variety)
3 cups boiling water
¼ teaspoon salt

Dry-roast the flakes in a cast-iron skillet for 5 minutes, shaking the pan occasionally to keep them from burning. You can use a capful of oil to roast them if desired, but this is unnecessary.

Add flakes to boiling water and then add salt; reduce flame and cover pan. Cook for about 30 minutes over an asbestos pad.

Baked Flakes
5 servings

3 cups wheat flakes
4 cups boiling water
½ teaspoon salt
1 cup sautéed vegetables (onions, carrots, cabbage)
1 tablespoon tamari

Toast wheat flakes as above and scald with boiling water; add salt. Pour half of the scalded flakes into a casserole dish, cover with vegetables, and add remaining flakes. Sprinkle top with tamari and cover casserole. Bake for 45 minutes in a 375° oven. Remove cover and bake another 15 minutes until the top is crisp.

Grain Milk or Kohkoh*

4 servings

Grain milk is a prepared food made from the flours of oats, sweet rice, soybeans, and brown rice plus ground sesame seeds. It is an excellent food for babies and may be prepared as a beverage or breakfast cereal. Kohkoh makes a good base for sweet puddings or dessert creams and is also good in muffin batters.

For thick cereal

1 cup grain milk powder	5 cups water
½ teaspoon oil	¼ teaspoon salt

For thin cereal or beverage

4 heaping tablespoons grain milk powder	4 cups water
¼ teaspoon oil	dash of salt

In a heavy 1½-quart saucepan sauté the powder in oil, stirring occasionally for about 5 minutes. Remove from heat and let pan cool for a few minutes. Add cold water gradually to prevent lumping. Add salt and return pan to stove and bring to a boil over a medium flame.

To reduce lumps, use a wire whisk to lightly beat the grain milk as it comes to a boil. Lower flame and cook over an asbestos pad until thick, stirring occasionally to prevent scorching.

For a thick cereal cook 30 to 40 minutes. The thinner milk is ready in about 15 or 20 minutes. Season with sesame salt or tamari.

Sprouts Made from Grain

Sprouts are not considered a regular part of the macrobiotic diet. However, they offer an easy way to have fresh greens in the winter and, cooked, can be a delicious addition to soups, sautéed vegetables, casseroles, or breads.

* Also called infant cereal or koko.

1 cup oats, wheat, barley, rye, or rice
large glass container
cheesecloth
rubber band or string
spring water for soaking (if using tap water, boil first for 10 minutes)

Wash grains carefully in cold water several times. Pick out any hulls or foreign matter. Place grain in a jar and cover with water. Cover top with cheesecloth and secure. Soak for at least 12 hours. Wheat berries need about 24 hours.

Leaving cover on jar, pour off soaking water. This water should not be discarded, but may be saved for making whole grain or soup. Rinse grains with fresh water and invert jar in a warm, dark place, allowing the air to circulate. For green sprouts, leave in a sunny spot after 48 hours.

Continue to rinse and drain two or three times a day. Some sprouts will be ready within 2 days, others may take as long as 5 or 6, depending upon the type of grain and the season.

Sprouts can also be made from beans. Soybeans, mung beans, etc., are easy to sprout following the same directions for making sprouts from grain.

Noodles

Noodles are the best way to eat flour. After whole grains, they are the easiest cereal to digest, easy to prepare, and lend themselves well to an endless variety of dishes. They can be added to soup during the last minutes of cooking, mixed with sautéed vegetables, or heated with hot water and served as a side dish.

Leftover noodles are fun to experiment with. Try cold noodles mixed in with a salad; deep-fry noodles and crumble to use as a garnish with vegetables, for casseroles, or fish; or mix with leftover cooked grain, smothered in sauce and baked as an entree.

Most supermarkets carry udon, a flat, hard, wheat noodle, in the Oriental food section. Soba noodles (made from buckwheat and sometimes with whole wheat) are fairly easy to find also. Whole wheat spaghetti and short macaroni noodles (both whole wheat and buckwheat) are carried in most health and natural food stores. Some imported varieties of Italian or Greek noodles are fairly pure; these are generally carried in smaller groceries. If you can't always get good quality noodles, try making your own.

Homemade Buckwheat Noodles

4 to 6 servings

½ teaspoon sea salt
1½ cups buckwheat flour
½ cup whole wheat flour
1 organic egg
cold water
extra flour for rolling noodles

Rub salt into flours with your hands in a large bowl. Break egg into the flour and stir with a rice paddle.

Add water slowly. How much water depends upon the size of the egg, hardness of the flour, etc. Dough should be soft but not wet.

Knead for about 10 minutes until the dough is elastic. Pat out on a well-floured board and roll from the center outward, trying to keep dough uniformly thick. When the dough is fairly thin, lightly dust surface with flour and roll up around a chopstick. Remove chopstick and slice crosswise into thin strips.

Drop into boiling water and cook for 10 minutes. Drain, saving water, and rinse in cold water.

Leftover water can be used for a broth by adding some scallions and/or parsley seasoned with tamari, and poured over noodles; or saved for soup stock, making breads, etc.

French Dumpling Strips

Makes about 2 dozen

Here is a noodle recipe that adds a special touch to soups and stews.

1 cup whole wheat pastry flour
¼ teaspoon sea salt
1½ tablespoons sesame oil
⅓ cup cold water
some corn flour and extra pastry flour for rolling dough
pinch or two of your favorite herb (optional)

Mix the dry ingredients in a bowl. Add the oil and rub into the flour, using just your fingertips. Slowly add the water and knead the dough thoroughly. Continue kneading for 10 minutes, until the dough is shiny and elastic.

Divide the dough in half and roll out, one section at a time, on a well-floured pastry board. When the dough reaches ¼-inch thickness cut into strips 1 inch wide and 2 inches long.

Dust each strip lightly with corn flour. *For soups:* Drop noodles into stock during the last 15 minutes of cooking.

For stews: Prepare noodles in advance. Cook in 2 quarts rapidly boiling water for 15 minutes. Drain in a strainer and rinse with cold water. Place in a bowl until ready to use. Add during the last few minutes of cooking time for stews or vegetables—just long enough to warm the noodles thoroughly.

These noodles are also good when served with a light miso sauce.

Breads and Other Things from Flour

THE AROMATIC SMELL of bread baking in the oven is a perfume that we often neglect to enjoy simply because it takes so long to make. When we do take the time to learn a few techniques, the mysterious art of making bread suddenly becomes easy, and we discover that there is no secret to creating something so basic.

Surprisingly, after the flour, one of the most important ingredients in making a loaf of bread that will rise naturally is water. As discussed before, pure water, either spring water or filtered tap water, is best. If pure water is not available,

Breads and Other Things from Flour 87

boil your tap water for 5 minutes to release some of the chemical compounds. Chlorine gas will be removed in the process, and calcium carbonate will be broken down to simple carbon dioxide, leaving a trace of calcium in the water.

Organically grown grains taste sweeter and make better breads when the flour is as fresh as possible. An inexpensive hand mill is a good investment if you plan to make your own breads frequently.

When grain is made into flour, some of the value of the grain is destroyed in the milling process. For this reason it is better to incorporate some whole-cooked grain in the dough; it makes the bread lighter and easier to digest.

Kneading bread brings out the gluten; this is the substance that makes the dough elastic and holds the loaf together. The more you knead, the more the texture of the bread will be improved. Finally, shaping the dough with a little water makes a lighter crust; the use of oil will make the crust a little heavier.

There are endless combinations of whole grains, flours, and slightly processed grains that can be used together to make fragrant breads that will rise naturally. Macrobiotic breads are made without commercial yeasting agents. In the following recipes you may use yeast if you wish, but remember that it is sugar-based and therefore very yin and should only be eaten occasionally.

Buckwheat flour is very heavy and should be used in small amounts when making bread. Whole wheat flour has the highest amount of gluten—for this reason it makes a dough that is rather sticky and is best used in combination with other flours. Rye flour is darker and heavier than wheat and does not rise well unless mixed with some other flour, such as wheat. Millet, oat, rice, barley, and corn flour can all be used in various proportions with wheat. Also, in summer you may want to add chestnut or soy flour to sweeten the dough.

A slow, steady oven temperature is necessary for a loaf that has a firm but soft crust and is completely cooked inside. A high temperature in the beginning of baking time will produce a hard crust that prevents the bread from being thoroughly baked. Brushing the top of a loaf with oil after the bread is halfway done will make a harder crust. Oil need not be used in making the dough.

In place of plain water, try using soup stocks, water used in cooking noodles, or tea. Instead of using salt, try sesame salt. For extra taste add seeds or nuts or a handful of chopped dried fruit.

Unyeasted Bread

Unyeasted bread is almost the only kind a macrobiotic cook prepares for her family. The basic recipes are simple to make and create an end product that is heavy and requires a lot of chewing. If you have a lazy jaw, it will be most unfortunate because the more these breads are chewed, the sweeter they become. Bread is a yang preparation of grain and uses much less water and longer cooking than whole grain. In the beginning, it may take your digestive system a while to adjust to this concentrated goodness—so don't overdo.

Basic Bread Doughs for Unyeasted Bread

I

2 cups whole wheat flour
1 cup buckwheat flour
1 cup corn flour or meal
1 teaspoon salt
2 cups water

II

2 cups wheat flour
1 cup barley flour
1 cup brown rice flour
4 teaspoons sesame salt
2 tablespoons corn oil
2 cups water

III

2 cups whole wheat flour
2 cups rye flour
1 teaspoon salt
½ teaspoon caraway seeds
2 cups water

Mix flours together with salt; add water gradually, stirring well. Knead dough 300 times. Place in an oiled bread pan and cover with a damp cloth; let rise several hours or overnight in a warm place. Bake 2 to 3 hours in a 300° to 325° oven.

Tips for a sweeter bread: Pan-roast flour in a dry skillet over a medium flame until flour darkens slightly and proceed as above. The addition of ½ cup soy, chestnut, or sweet rice flour will also sweeten dough. Up to 1 tablespoon of oil can be added for each cup of flour for a more moist loaf.

Breads and Other Things from Flour

In our house we like breads that have a lot of whole cooked grain added to the dough. The following recipe is for a light bread that is especially good to bake in spring or summer.

Whole Rice Bread

2 cups cooked brown rice*
2 cups liquid (leftover noodle water, bancha or mu tea, etc.)
2 cups whole wheat flour
½ cup barley or corn flour
½ teaspoon sea salt
1 tablespoon sesame oil
1 to 2 cups extra flour
oil for bread pan

Place rice in a bowl, pour over liquid, and break up rice with a rice paddle. Stir in 2 cups whole wheat flour. Pan-roast the barley flour in a skillet for a few minutes and add to batter. Mix in salt and oil and knead batter with rice paddle for 10 minutes.

Cover bowl with a damp towel and let rise for 6 hours. Remove towel, mix in remaining flour with your hands until dough is soft and elastic.

Place dough in an oiled bread pan and shape into a loaf with wet hands. Let sit another hour before placing in a 300° oven for 2½ hours.

For variety, add ¼ cup toasted sesame seeds, or ½ cup currants that have been boiled in water for a few minutes.

Rice Kayu

Rice kayu is very soft rice that has been puréed through a food mill. It makes a good leavening agent for breads when allowed to sit 8 hours or more before being added to bread dough.

There are two methods of preparation. Either cook rice, following the directions for porridge, using 5 to 7 parts water and a small amount of salt, or add an equal amount of cooked rice (which has been prepared with 2 to 3 times as much water) to water and simmer for 20 minutes or more. Put either preparation through a food mill, adding the pulp to the puréed cream, if desired. Leftover bran can be used in other batters, soups, or for croquettes.

* In place of rice and water, 4 cups of rice kayu can be used.

Whole Wheat Bread with Millet
Makes 1 loaf

4 cups wheat berries
6 cups water
¾ teaspoon salt
2 cups cooked millet
4 tablespoons toasted sesame seeds
oil for bread pan

Wash wheat berries several times in cold water. Place in a large bowl, cover with water, place a layer of cheesecloth on top to keep out dust, and let soak for 24 hours.

Drain berries, reserving soaking water. Grind through a hand grain mill. The cracked grain will come out in dough form—very sticky and thick. (For easiest cleaning, wash mill immediately after grinding berries in cold water.)

Add salt to the wheat, knead for 15 minutes, add millet and sesame seeds, and knead for another 10 minutes. If dough is too stiff, add some of the soaking water. Shape bread into a loaf (dipping your fingers in cold water will prevent sticking), place in an oiled bread pan, and let rise in a warm place for 3 to 6 hours. Bake in a slow oven, 275° to 300°, for 3 to 4 hours.

VARIATIONS: If desired, 1 to 2 cups flour can be added to dough, or millet can be replaced by another cooked grain, such as rice, oats, or barley. One-half cup of toasted cornmeal, scalded with 1 cup cooking water added to dough, is another pleasant variation. Chopped nuts, dried fruit, or ½ cup raw grated carrot can be added for extra taste.

Corn Spoon Bread
Makes 9 squares

2 cups cornmeal
3 cups boiling water
1 cup whole wheat flour
2 cups cooked brown rice
3 tablespoons corn germ oil
¾ teaspoon sea salt
¼ cup soy or chestnut flour (optional)
1 to 2 eggs (optional)
2 tablespoons roasted sesame seeds

Roast cornmeal in a dry cast-iron skillet over a high flame for about 7 minutes, stirring constantly to prevent burning. When the corn begins to darken pour into a large mixing bowl and scald with the boiling water. Mix lightly and let the cornmeal swell for about 10 minutes before adding the other ingredients.

Beat in all the other ingredients, except for the sesame seeds, and spoon into a shallow, oiled casserole dish or 9x12 cake pan, and sprinkle with sesame seeds. Bake 40 minutes in a 375° oven.

For variety, add 1 cup cooked sweet corn or sautéed vegetables to batter.

For muffins, add ½ cup whole wheat pastry flour and bake at 375° for 30 to 40 minutes. Blueberries or boiled currants can be added for a sweeter taste.

For corn fritters, omit oil from recipe; drop batter a spoonful at a time into hot oil, and deep-fry until browned and crisp.

Chapatis

Chapatis are the flat, pancake-shaped breads that are a staple food of the people living in many parts of Asia. In India they are made with a coarse wheat flour that can be imitated by using a combination of unbleached white or pastry flour with whole wheat flour.

Basic Dough
Makes 6 chapatis

1 cup flour
½ teaspoon salt

¼ to ⅓ cup water, approximately

Place flour in a shallow mixing bowl and rub salt into the grain; add water gradually and knead the dough until it feels as soft as your earlobe. Roll dough into small balls, less than 1 inch in diameter; then place them one at a time on a well-floured board, flatten slightly with your palm, and roll out to a 6-inch diameter. If you don't have a rolling pin, just coat a glass bottle or jar with flour and use it to roll out dough.

To pan-fry: Brush both sides of chapatis with oil and cook over a high flame until crisp and slightly browned. To bake: Oil a cookie sheet and bake for 15 minutes in a preheated 350° oven.

VARIATIONS: A teaspoon or more of oil may be added for each cup of flour for a slightly richer taste. Or try making puri: roll out dough to 3-inch circles and deep-fry by dropping them one at a time in hot oil and holding them under the oil with a spatula until they begin to puff up. Release and let them rise, turning when one side is browned. Cook a few more seconds until the other side is browned, then remove with an oil strainer and drain on brown paper or toweling.

For crackers: Roll dough out directly onto an oiled cookie sheet. Score the entire surface into 2-inch squares with a wet knife, sprinkle with sesame seeds, and bake in a 350° oven for 15 to 20 minutes. Makes about 2 dozen crackers.

Pancakes, Crepes, and Waffles

Buckwheat Crepes

12 crepes

1 cup buckwheat flour
3 cups water
¼ teaspoon salt
1 egg (optional)
oil for frying

Mix all ingredients in a bowl. If you are not using an egg, let batter sit for several hours or overnight to thicken.

Brush a skillet or griddle lightly with oil and heat. When the griddle is hot, pour in a thin layer of batter quickly. It helps to use a soup ladle to pour just the right amount of batter. Do not turn the pancake until it is set and the edges are crisp. Fry on both sides.

For the main course, fill pancakes with vegetables, roll up and serve with rice and béchamel sauce. For dessert, spread pancakes with apple butter, applesauce, or puréed chestnuts, and sprinkle with raisins.

Whole Wheat Pancakes

12 pancakes

1 cup whole wheat flour (or whole wheat pastry flour)
¼ teaspoon salt
1 tablespoon oil
2¼ cups water

Prepare as for the buckwheat crepes.

For dessert crepes, 1 tablespoon of soybean flour or chestnut flour may be added to sweeten batter, along with ½ teaspoon of cinnamon and/or an organic egg. Fresh grated apples are also good added directly to the batter just before cooking.

Waffles

Makes 6 waffles

½ cup buckwheat flour
½ cup whole wheat flour
½ cup sweet rice flour
1 tablespoon oil

2 cups water
¾ teaspoon salt
1 egg (optional)
extra oil for waffle pan

Mix dry ingredients; add oil, water, and salt. Beat with a wire whisk or hand beater until batter is light and full of air. Heat the waffle iron and pour in batter. Waffles take between 8 to 10 minutes to cook.

VARIATIONS: Chestnut, soybean flour, barley, or oat flour may all be used in place of the sweet rice flour. Whole-cooked grain may also be added to the batter for an extra chewy taste. Or try adding fresh grated carrot or apple to the batter. For a summer dessert, this recipe is delicious when fresh mashed blueberries are folded into batter just before pouring on waffle iron.

For a main course, these waffles can be served with a miso spread, or for a dessert, serve with applesauce or apple butter and a sprinkle of cinnamon. Or, in summer, try a fresh fruit topping.

Oat Flakes Crust

Makes 2 thick crusts

3 cups oat flakes, dry-roasted for a few minutes
1½ cups rice flour
¼ cup cold pressed corn or sesame oil

1 tablespoon sesame seeds
¼ teaspoon oil
1 to 1¼ cups water

Dry-roast flakes in a hot skillet for a few minutes until they are lightly browned. Mix with dry ingredients. Add oil and knead. Slowly mix in water. This dough is very soft and does not need to be rolled out. Simply press into pie pan.

For best results let dough rest at least 30 minutes before kneading to allow flakes to absorb water.

Wheat, rye, or millet flakes can be used in combination or in place of oat flakes.

Whole Rice Crust
Makes 1 crust

1 cup cooked brown rice
1¾ cups flour
¼ teaspoon salt
¼ cup oil
4 to 5 tablespoons cold water

Purée rice in a blender or food mill. If rice is hard or dry, first boil in a small amount of water or steam to soften. Place rice in a bowl and knead flour into the grain. Add salt and oil and knead for just a few minutes. Roll out on a well-floured board.

This crust is especially good as a bottom crust for vegetable pies, or pies that are served as part of the main course.

The following is an all-purpose dough recipe that may be used for making vegetable pies, knishes, stuffed vegetable rolls, or plain cookies.

Kneaded Dough
Makes 2 crusts or 2 dozen knishes

4 cups flour (whole wheat, or a mixture of wheat, barley, oats, corn, or millet flour)
¾ teaspoon salt
4 tablespoons oil
1⅓ to 1½ cups water

Mix dry ingredients well. Add oil and rub into flour with your fingers until dough resembles a fine meal. Add water slowly and knead into dough. Continue to knead for a few more minutes until all ingredients hold together. Excess kneading will toughen dough.

Roll out on a lightly floured board to desired thickness.

Dessert Pie Dough
Makes 1 crust

2 cups whole wheat flour (or a combination of whole wheat and whole wheat pastry, or unbleached white flour)
¼ teaspoon salt
⅓ cup oil
grated orange or lemon rind (optional)
few tablespoons cold water
extra flour for rolling

Mix dry ingredients, add oil and rub into dough. Add water slowly, while continuing to mix and knead. Add grated rind. When dough holds together, roll out on a floured board.

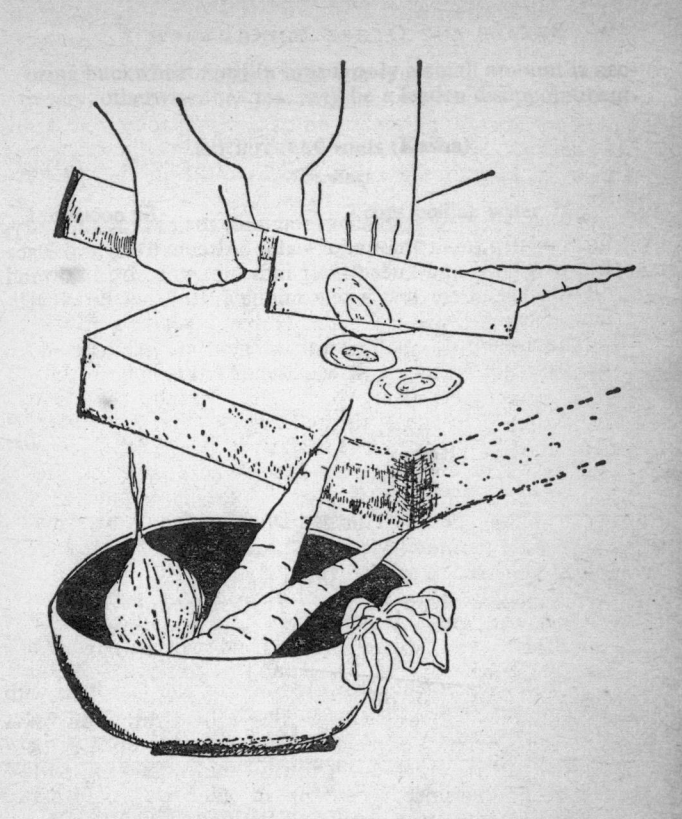

The Vegetables — Our Secondary Foods

ALTHOUGH vegetables provide us with valuable vitamins, minerals, carbohydrates, proteins, and fats, they fall into a group of secondary foods, after grains. Vegetables and fruits are not considered ideal foods by macrobiotics because of the separation between the fruit and the seed of the plant. With grains, the fruit and the seed are contained in one tiny compacted form with a much greater life force and energy potential.

We therefore place garden and sea vegetables, legumes and fruits, and animal products as side dishes on our table to complement the main attraction. There are no set percentages on what one should eat, but we try to maintain a ratio of at least 50 percent grain to the other foods. Generally, cooked vegetables comprise about half of the remaining amount, with the other foods found in decreasing amounts.

When we prepare vegetables, we apply the idea of yin and yang in selection, cutting, and cooking. Although any vegetables that grow within a 500-mile radius of your home may be eaten freely according to season, the three vegetables that are virtually excluded from a macrobiotic person's diet are potatoes, tomatoes, and eggplant. These are all basically extremely yin tropical plants which man has only been cultivating for a comparatively short time. The ratio of sodium to potassium in a potato, for instance, is about 3 to 400; it would be very difficult to try to balance this with other foods. For the same reasons, we try to avoid other tropical vegetables and fruits. However, if you are living in or move to a warmer, more tropical climate, such foods would be somewhat more in harmony with your environment, but they are not recommended as part of your daily foods.

Fresh organic vegetables are scrubbed with a special vegetable brush called a tawashi (available in Oriental and natural food stores) which is made from sea vegetation. All washing is done quickly in cold water to preserve nutrients and the life energy of foods.

In cutting vegetables we try to follow the natural order of the plant's growth. We usually start at the top, which is the most yin part, and cut down toward the more yang part, the root. For instance, in cutting an onion we would first cut it in half, then place each half flat on the cutting board and follow the natural divisions, cutting each section into thin crescents. In cutting carrots, we start at the top, slicing on the diagonal down toward the tip in thin pieces. By cutting on the diagonal, each part of the carrot is represented in a uniform cross-section. This is a simple and practical means of preparation for uniform cooking and taste.

For fast cooking or dishes where we want tiny morsels of carrots for garnish and seasoning, diagonal slices are stacked and cut into matchstick pieces.

When preparing several vegetables together, try to keep in mind the idea of balance. It is best to combine a vegetable that grows above the ground (a more yin, green leafy vegetable) with one that grows at ground level, or beneath the earth (a more yang, root vegetable). Combinations

Vegetables should be cut from yin ▽ to yang △, according to the way they are found growing.

Cut onions in half, then slice into crescents.

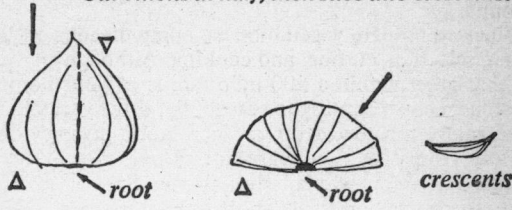

crescents

For carrots, cut on the diagonal, starting at the top; for matchstick pieces, stack and cut lengthwise.

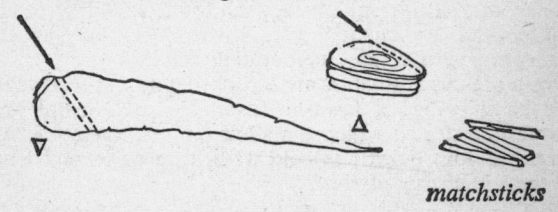

matchsticks

should be harmonious in color and texture as well as balanced in their components of yin and yang. Above all, try to avoid a chaotic potpourri of different foods at every meal. Simple cooking is easier to prepare and digest, and helps to keep your thinking clear.

To sauté vegetables, use a small amount of oil in a skillet. Just a capful or two is usually sufficient. Over a high flame, add the most yin vegetables first. We almost always cook onions first because this way the strong acids are released and the onion flavor does not overpower the other foods. Stir quickly and lightly, almost tossing the pieces for a few minutes before adding the next vegetable. This way each vegetable gets lightly coated with oil, and its own flavor is sealed in.

There are two basic methods in sautéing. In the first method, for fast cooking, or what is called stir-frying, vegetables are cut into thin pieces and sautéed over a high flame for 10 minutes. The flame is then reduced to medium height and stirring is continued for another 10 or 15 minutes. Seasoning with tamari and a little water is done at the end of cooking.

In the second method, the first 10 minutes of cooking are identical with the first method, except that the vegetables may be cut in larger pieces. After the sautéing, a small amount of water is added, and the pan is covered while the vegetables cook another 30 to 40 minutes. If salt is added at the beginning of cooking, the vegetables will retain a bright color, take less time to cook, but not become as tender. Salt added halfway through cooking will allow the vegetables to become tender. If seasoning, in the form of salt or tamari, is done near the end of cooking, vegetables will be tasty, but salt added at this time is slightly harder for the body to absorb.

The fascinating thing about this whole procedure of vegetable preparation is the colorful transformation that occurs in the cooking. Vegetables become much brighter and glisten in their pots. Provided that they are treated delicately, they will respond with a beautiful color, aroma, and taste.

Other methods, such as pressure cooking, steaming, baking, and boiling, are used occasionally in our vegetable cooking, but not nearly as extensively as sautéing. The most important thing to remember about sautéing is the amount of oil—sauté means sauté—not deep-fry!

Broccoli

Broccoli is a delicate vegetable that needs very little cooking. Overcooking will cause the tender flowerettes to lose their color and become watery. The whole plant may be used. After rinsing, just cut off the tip of the stem. Peel the stalk if it is fibrous, and slice it into thin pieces on the diagonal. Separate the flowerettes with a sharp knife.

For boiled broccoli, bring ¼ cup water to a boil; cook the stalk pieces first for 5 minutes, then add the tops and a pinch of salt. Cover and let steam over low heat for 10 minutes.

For sautéed broccoli, brush the bottom of a skillet with a small amount of oil and sauté the stems first for a few minutes, then add the flowerettes. Sauté a few more minutes; add a dash of salt, cover, and let steam for 15 minutes or until tender. Broccoli combines well with sliced Spanish onions and carrots, summer squash, or fresh sweet corn. It is very delicious simmered or baked in béchamel sauce. (See p. 158.)

Brussels Sprouts

Brussels sprouts may be cooked whole, boiled, steamed, or sautéed. A small cut in the base of the sprout will help it to cook uniformly. The outer leaves need not be discarded unless they are very yellow. Pressure cooking tends to turn these vegetables into a mushy pulp. After full pressure has been reached, you must be very careful to remove the cooker from heat after two minutes of cooking, and bring the pressure down immediately under cold water. Sprouts are very good sautéed with onions.

Burdock

Gardeners know burdock as a member of the aster family, while macrobiotic people know it as a plant with a white meaty root that grows abundantly in the wild state and is delicious to eat. Oriental and natural food stores carry a domesticated garden variety of burdock, but it is rather expensive, ranging anywhere from eighty cents to a dollar or more per pound. However, if you've ever taken the time to dig your own, you know that the wild varieties are just as good, or even better. In his excellent book, *Stalking the Wild Asparagus,* * author Euell Gibbons describes the techniques of searching and digging for burdock, as well as a wealth of information for gathering other wild plants.

Stored in a box of sand, burdock roots will keep all year round. However, if you are lacking storage space, you will want to dry them this way. Scrub the roots thoroughly and slice on the diagonal into pieces ½ inch thick. Place on a cake rack or cookie sheet to dry, spreading pieces so they are not touching each other. Turn over daily. A piece of cheesecloth can be placed over the burdock to keep out dust. We use these chips in stews and soups, soaking them several hours before cooking and using the soaking water in the cooking.

* Euell Gibbons, *Stalking the Wild Asparagus* (David McKay, 1966).

Chips roasted in a slow oven for several hours and infused with boiling water make a delicious tea. Stored chips keep best if stored in airtight glass containers.

Burdock is a very yang, tough, root vegetable that requires more cooking than other vegetables. It can be prepared either by slicing crosswise into thin rounds, or by slicing into thin slivers, as if you were sharpening a pencil. It combines well with onions, carrots, and hiziki seaweed, and is also a tasty addition to soups. Since the flavor is quite unlike any other vegetable, it may take a while to acquire a passion for it. Properly prepared, it can be delicious.

Burdock and Salted Plums
5 servings

(This is one of the quickest ways to prepare burdock. It is also one of the most palatable and has a pleasing sweet-sour taste.)

1 pound fresh burdock roots	2 or 3 umeboshi salt plums
	water

Scrub the roots thoroughly. Do not remove the dark outer skin. Cut each root into 2-inch pieces on the diagonal.

For pressure cooking, use ¼ cup water. Place burdock, plums, and water in a pressure cooker and bring up to full pressure over a high flame. Reduce flame as soon as full pressure is reached and cook over a medium flame for 8 minutes. Remove from heat and let pressure drop.

For regular cooking, boil 1 cup of water in a saucepan, add plums and burdock, and reduce flame. Cover and let simmer for 30 to 40 minutes, or until burdock is soft and easily pierced with a fork.

Leftover liquid may be used in soup or sauce.

For other recipes using burdock, see index.

Sautéed Green Vegetables
4 servings

1 small head cabbage, *or* 1 pound kale, Swiss chard, beet or turnip greens	2 teaspoons oil water

Separate the leaves and rinse carefully in cold water to remove any soil or bugs. In summer, bugs are quite common in organic vegetables, so look each leaf over carefully. Place leaves together, one on top of the other, and cut vertically down the main stem, then cut into 1-inch strips following the ribs of the leaves.

Sauté pieces in a preheated wok or skillet with the oil for about 5 minutes, tossing gently. Add just a small amount of water (a few tablespoons) to prevent leaves from sticking to pan and season with 1 tablespoon tamari or ¼ teaspoon sea salt. Cover and let steam for 10 to 15 minutes.

Carrots

Carrots are delicious by themselves whether baked, steamed, boiled, or sautéed. They combine well with just about any combination of vegetables, and are especially good when sautéed with sea vegetables.

Carrots and Burdock

2 to 3 servings

2 burdock roots	⅛ teaspoon salt
4 carrots	1 tablespoon tamari
1 teaspoon oil	

After scrubbing the burdock roots, shave with a sharp knife as if you were sharpening a pencil. Cut scrubbed carrots into thin slivers.

Heat oil in a skillet and sauté the burdock until it begins to change color; toss aside and sauté carrots for a few minutes. Add just enough water to cover the bottom of the pan, cover, and let steam for 15 minutes. Add salt and continue to cook for another 20 minutes. Add tamari and cook another 5 minutes.

Carrots and Watercress

4 servings

2 teaspoons oil	2 to 3 carrots, cut into matchstick pieces
3 or 4 scallions, cut into ½-inch pieces	sea salt
1 bunch watercress, washed and chopped	approximately 1 tablespoon tamari

Sauté the scallions in a skillet preheated with the oil. Push to the side of the pan and add the watercress. As soon as the color of the watercress brightens add the carrots and continue to sauté for another 5 minutes. Add a dash of salt and cover; let cook for about 10 minutes over a low heat.

Sprinkle with about 1 tablespoon of tamari and continue to cook for 5 to 10 minutes.

This preparation is almost like a salad and very refreshing in summer or spring. For variety, add a few spoonfuls of roasted sesame or sunflower seeds, or use a shredded umeboshi plum in place of the salt. A tablespoon of sesame butter can also be added after cooking and lightly mixed in as a dressing.

Carrots and Sea Vegetables
5 servings

2 pieces of kombu seaweed *or* 1½ ounces of nato kombu or hiziki seaweed
1 tablespoon oil
1 onion, thinly sliced

3 large carrots, sliced thinly on the diagonal
2 to 3 tablespoons tamari
2 teaspoons sesame seeds

Rinse seaweed in cold water and soak with 2 cups of water in a deep bowl for at least 15 minutes. Squeeze excess liquid from hiziki or nato kombu. If using kombu, cut into thin strips ½ inch wide and an inch long.

First sauté the onion in a small amount of oil. After a few minutes, push the pieces aside and add the seaweed. After 2 or 3 more minutes, add the carrots and continue to sauté for another 5 minutes. Pour in about half of the soaking water. Sand and other foreign matter will have sunk to the bottom of the bowl, so be careful not to let these go into the pot.

Bring vegetables to a boil, lower flame and let simmer for 5 minutes. Add sesame seeds and tamari, and cover pan, leaving lid slightly ajar so steam can escape.

Let simmer for another 30 minutes, adding more soaking water if necessary. This preparation should be slightly salty; taste it; if it isn't, season with another tablespoon or two of tamari.

Cauliflower

Cauliflower may be prepared and cooked in the same way as broccoli. We find it tastes best sautéed; this way the delicate flavor is not lost. It is especially good served with an onion béchamel sauce (see p. 159), or used in tempura (see p. 109). Also, lightly boiled flowerettes make a nice addition to salad. Do not discard the outer leaves; they are very mild and taste delicious cooked by any method.

Dandelion Greens

Dandelion leaves should be picked from tender, young plants, preferably those found growing in open fields away from roads. The inner leaves are less bitter than the outer ones.

Crunchy Cabbage
6 servings

¼ cup seeds (sesame, pumpkin, or sunflower)
1 teaspoon oil
3 scallions, minced, *or* 2 tablespoons chopped chives
1 green cabbage, shredded
¼ teaspoon salt
2 tablespoons tamari

Heat a wok or large skillet and toast seeds over a high flame, stirring constantly. When seeds begin to pop, add oil and scallions or chives. Cook for 2 minutes, tossing frequently; add cabbage and sauté for 5 minutes.

Season with salt and tamari and continue to toss vegetables and cook for another 5 to 10 minutes.

VARIATIONS: This basic recipe can also be tried with other green leafy vegetables, such as Chinese or celery cabbage, watercress, or spinach.

Sautéed Dandelion Greens
5 servings

1 pound fresh dandelion leaves
1 teaspoon sesame or sunflower oil
⅛ teaspoon salt

Chop the leaves into small pieces and sauté in oil for about 10 minutes. Add a tiny amount of water with the salt and cover. Let steam over a low heat for 20 to 30 more minutes. Tamari may be added near the end of cooking for extra taste.

Dandelion greens, like watercress, are rather strong; they may be used interchangeably in many recipes.

Boston, Iceberg, and Romaine Lettuce

All types of lettuce taste wonderful when lightly sautéed. They are good all by themselves as a vegetable when prepared this way.

Sautéed Lettuce

4 servings

1 head lettuce
2 teaspoons oil (olive or sunflower oil tastes best)
salt and tamari for seasoning

Cut lettuce into quarters and sauté in a preheated wok or skillet for a few minutes with the oil. Toss constantly, and at the last minute add a dash of salt and/or a few drops of tamari for seasoning.

Roasted sesame, pumpkin, or sunflower seeds are a nice addition to this preparation. Fresh chopped parsley or chives also makes an attractive garnish.

Endive may be prepared in the same way.

The Onion Family

Did you know that chives, garlic, leeks, scallions and shallots are all members of the lily family and closely related to the well-known bulb onion? In our cooking, we tend to avoid the more yin purple onion and use the white or yellow onion frequently. In combining onions with other vegetables, even with those more yin types, the onions are sautéed first to release oxalic acid, which tends to overpower the other foods and hampers digestion.

Onions are rich in minerals and serve as cleansing agents in removing toxins from the body. Chives, scallions, and shallots are more yin than bulb onions, and are used more as a garnish than a vegetable in our cooking. A touch of garlic adds a nice accent to almost all vegetables, provided it is used sparingly.

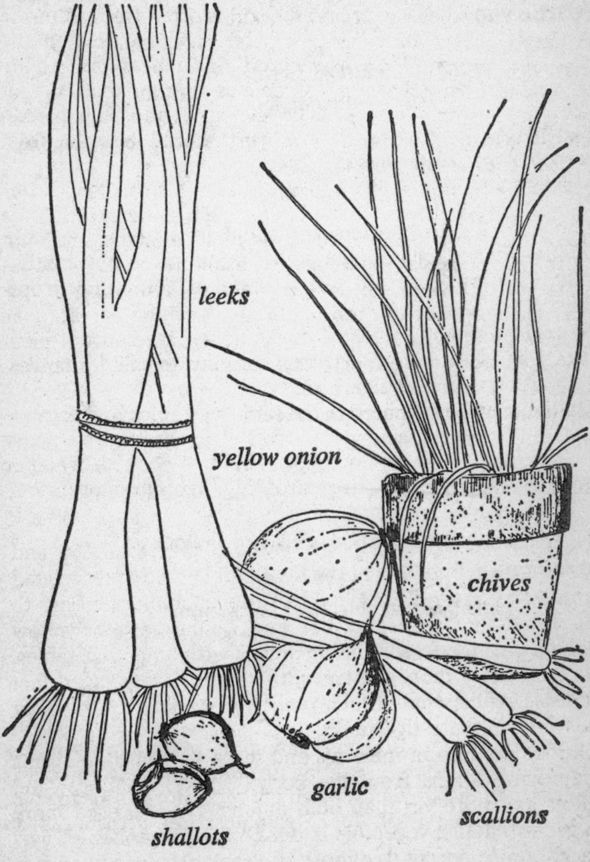
leeks
yellow onion
chives
garlic
scallions
shallots

Sautéed Leeks

3 to 4 servings

3 to 4 leeks
¼ teaspoon oil

pinch of salt

Leeks tend to be sandy and the soil is often trapped inside the long leaves. After rinsing off the vegetable, cut off the white end. Separate the leaves and rinse them thoroughly under cold running water to remove foreign matter. Cut greens into ½-inch pieces. Slice the bulb into thin pieces. The roots are also quite good and should also be used chopped into small pieces.

Heat the oil in a skillet and add the bulb slices first. After they have cooked for a few minutes, push aside and add the greens. Continue to sauté for a few more minutes, and then add the roots. Lower the flame, cover and let cook for about 15 minutes. Then add the salt, and a small amount of water if the leeks appear dry, and continue cooking for another 15 to 20 minutes.

Cooked leeks are a marvelous addition to salad, noodles, or sauce.

Parsnips are extremely sweet root vegetables and may be prepared in the same way as carrots. They are more starchy than carrots, however, and should be well cooked, whether they are prepared by baking, steaming, or in tempura.

Creamed Parsnips and Onions

4 servings

1 pound parsnips, scrubbed clean
1 pound yellow onions
1 teaspoon oil
⅛ teaspoon sea salt
1 cup water

Slice parsnips into thin pieces on the diagonal. Cut onions in half, then into thin slivers.

For pressure cooking, sauté onions in oil for a few minutes before adding parsnips. Add ¼ cup water and salt and bring cooker up to full pressure; when the regulator begins to spin, lower flame and cook for 5 minutes. Let pressure drop normally.

For regular cooking, sauté vegetables as above. Add water and bring vegetables to a boil, then reduce flame and cover. After about 15 minutes add salt and cook for another 20 minutes, or until parsnips are very soft.

For a creamy consistency, mash vegetables with a fork. For an extra protein kick, a spoonful of kome miso may be mixed into vegetables.

Spinach in Cream Sauce
5 to 6 servings

2 pounds fresh spinach leaves	3 tablespoons flour
1 cup water	⅛ teaspoon salt
1 tablespoon oil	2 tablespoons tamari

Wash leaves several times under cold running water to remove any soil particles. Place on a cutting board and chop into ½-inch pieces.

Boil water in a large skillet or wok and add salt and spinach. Let spinach simmer uncovered for 5 minutes, stirring constantly.

Turn off heat, cover pan, and set aside. In a one-quart saucepan heat oil. Add flour and stir constantly over a low heat for 3 minutes. Remove from stove and let cool for a few minutes.

Strain spinach cooking juice into the saucepan while stirring constantly to prevent lumping. Return to stove and simmer for about 10 minutes, stirring occasionally. Add spinach leaves and tamari and simmer together for 10 more minutes.

Succotash—American Indian Misickquatash
6 servings

4 ears sweet corn, husked	2 teaspoons oil
1 pound zucchini	2 cups cooked red beans
1 sweet green or red pepper, deseeded	few pinches of sea salt

Scrape kernels off corn as close to the cob as possible. Dice zucchini and pepper into small pieces. Sauté the pepper and zucchini in the oil for about 5 minutes. Add corn, beans, and salt. Cook over a low flame for about 10 to 15 minutes, stirring constantly. A few drops of tamari may be added near the end of cooking.

This combination is great with noodles, couscous, millet, or rice. The extra oil makes the beans more digestible.

Baked Turnips

3 to 4 servings

3 to 4 large turnips　　　　1 capful oil
1 tablespoon tamari

Scrub the turnips thoroughly and cut off stump left from stem. Cut into quarters and sprinkle with tamari. Place in a casserole brushed lightly with oil, cover, and bake in a 375° oven for 40 to 50 minutes.

VARIATIONS: Use various combinations of other vegetables, such as carrots and onions, Italian squash, parsnips, etc.

Baked Squash

4 to 6 servings (depending on size of squash)

1 large butternut, acorn, or　　oil
　　Hubbard squash　　　　　water
salt

Scrub the outside of the squash thoroughly. Cut squash into about 6 pieces, scoop out seeds, and reserve. Sprinkle each piece with salt and rub it into the flesh with your fingers. Brush the surface with oil. Replace the seeds over each piece (to seal in moisture) and arrange in a cake pan or casserole. Pour in enough water to make a ¼ to ½ inch depth. Cover pan. Bake in a 400° oven for 45 to 60 minutes, checking occasionally to see that water does not boil away.

If you prefer to roast the seeds, rinse and strain them after separating them from the fibrous material. Place on a cookie sheet or pie pan and sprinkle with tamari. Roast in a warm oven (350°) until they begin to pop.

Tempura

TEMPURA is a Japanese term for vegetables or other foods that are dipped into a special batter and deep-fried. The batters suggested here are to be used more or less as a guide, for the fun of making tempura depends upon how widely you want to experiment.

For a successful batter, just mix the ingredients lightly; too much mixing will bring out the gluten in the wheat flour and create a sticky batter. Lumps don't matter, so don't worry about making a smooth mixture.

Chill vegetables and batter beforehand, and give the batter a quick stir before use. Always use oil that is hot and at least several inches deep at the center of the pan or wok. At first the vegetables will sink to the bottom and then float to the top of the bubbling oil—so be sure not to do too many vegetables at the same time so they will all have room to move freely. Some vegetables need to be turned over; wait until one side is lightly brown or deep golden before turning.

When doing a large amount of tempura for dinner, it helps to place the cooked vegetables on a cookie sheet lined with brown paper or paper towels, or on a wire rack, and set in a warm oven until you are ready to serve. This way the vegetables will remain crisp and hot.

Leftover oil should be strained through cheesecloth into a clean glass jar. An umeboshi plum placed with the oil will prevent it from becoming rancid. Tempura oil can be used over and over again if treated this way until it begins to lose its properties. About two months is the maximum time for keeping used oil if you store it in the refrigerator.

It is very important to use salt in making the batter—salt attracts the hot oil so that the vegetables are quickly cooked. Serve a dip* with the tempura to enhance the taste and aid digestion. If you don't have time to make a dip, serve with some tamari diluted with a little water or tea. To make tempura you will need:

vegetables, scrubbed and cut into large, thin pieces on the diagonal

chopsticks or an oil strainer
about 1 quart of sunflower or soya oil

Tempura Batters

Each of the following recipes makes enough tempura batter to cover approximately 18 pieces of vegetable.

I

1 cup whole wheat flour (or pastry flour for fruits)
1¼ cups water

1 tablespoon arrowroot starch
½ teaspoon salt

II

½ cup corn flour
½ cup whole wheat or pastry flour

½ teaspoon salt
1 or 1¼ cups water

III

½ cup unbleached white flour
½ cup whole wheat or pastry flour

1 egg
1 cup water
½ teaspoon salt

* See p. 160 for tempura dips.

Have all vegetables cut in advance.

Extra flour if needed.

Don't over-mix batter.

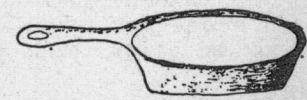

Use a heavy skillet or a wok.

A cookie sheet and paper towels or a wire rack can be used for draining excess oil.

Oil strainer

112 TEMPURA

VARIATIONS FOR BATTERS: For fruit tempura, add some grated cinnamon or nutmeg to the batter and use a little apple juice in place of the water. Barley, sweet rice flour, millet, or oat flour are also very good to use. Or replace part of the grain flour with a small amount of soy or chestnut flour.

Buckwheat flour is also very good, but heavy, so use only a small amount.

DIRECTIONS

Cut vegetables in advance and chill. Some vegetables, like lotus root or other vegetables with a high water content, should be sprinkled lightly with salt and allowed to drain for 15 minutes before using.

Use chopsticks to dip vegetables into batter and then into oil. If the batter seems to slide off the vegetables, dust them first with a little arrowroot starch or a mixture of starch and whole wheat flour so the batter will adhere better. Always drain tempura on a rack or paper before serving.

Most vegetables take only a few minutes to cook, depending upon the thickness and the type of flour used. Green leafy vegetables take only about a minute.

SUGGESTED VEGETABLES TO TRY:

Whole watercress, beet or turnip tops, parsley, cauliflower (leaves and tops), butternut, acorn, or yellow squash (cut into strips), zucchini, cucumber, carrot, onion rings, turnips, parsnips, broccoli, green peppers, celery tops, carrot tops, string beans, kale or Swiss chard.

OR TRY FRUIT:

Apples cut into circles, peach slices, apricots, bananas (very yin, however).

Some Additional Notes on Tempura

If the oil becomes cloudy or full of little particles, drop an umeboshi plum into the pan and let it cook for several minutes, or until it becomes charred. It will attract all the excess materials. Remove plum and continue to fry other vegetables.

Tempura always looks attractive when served on a leaf or two of vegetable greens or garnished with sprigs of fresh parsley. For color, add chopped fresh chives to tempura dip. Leftover pieces of fried batter are good in soups and casseroles.

Use extra batter the next day for pancakes or making deep-fried grain croquettes: mix about ½ cup cooked whole grain or bulgar or couscous with just enough batter to bind mixture. Compress into small balls, sprinkle with tamari, and fry. Croquettes are especially good when stuffed with small amounts of sautéed vegetables or hiziki seaweed.

For vegetable dumplings, grate raw carrot, or other root vegetable, with a little cabbage and mix lightly into batter; add whole cooked grains if desired. Drop by spoonfuls into hot oil and remove when golden brown. These are very good in soup.

Salads

SALADS offer a bright note to a meal. In our cooking, pressed salads are prepared and eaten more often than raw salads.* Pressing vegetables with salt tends to make them more yang—the liquids are reduced and the acidity of the raw foods is neutralized. A pressed salad is a delicate blend of flavors and only small portions—just a couple of tablespoons—are served to each person.

Pressed Salad

6 servings

2 heads lettuce or Chinese cabbage
1 carrot, grated
1 bunch radishes (greens included), thinly sliced
½ tablespoon sea salt or a few umeboshi salt plums

Cut lettuce or cabbage leaves into 1-inch pieces. Mix all ingredients in a large salad bowl, add salt, and toss vegetables with your fingers to blend. If using umeboshi plums, shred flesh from pits† and rub into vegetables.

Japanese salad presses are available in many Oriental and natural food outlets. If you have such a press, place vegtables inside it and turn the handle on top just enough to slightly press the vegetables. Continue to give the handle a turn every few hours as the juices are expelled. Do not pour off the juice, for it helps in the pressing of the vegetables.

If you don't have a press, place vegetables in a bowl and

---

* Eating raw organic food may cause parasites; for this reason heating pressed salads for a few minutes before serving is recommended.

† Don't throw away the pits—a tender, edible nutmeat lies inside and can be retrieved with a nutcracker.

use a plate weighted with a heavy rock or brick. The salad can be eaten after a few hours but tastes best when pressed one or two days. This type of salad can be eaten year round.

Variations on this basic recipe are endless. Some other good combinations are: Cucumber–radish–carrot; cabbage–carrot–scallion; turnip–carrot–cabbage; watercress–carrot–apple; watercress–celery–radish; zucchini–carrot–onion; lettuce–green pepper–carrot; Swiss chard–onion–carrot.

Summer Salad

6 to 8 servings

1 small head cabbage, shredded	1 tablespoon sea salt
2 apples, grated (skin included if organic)	¼ cup currants, boiled for a few minutes in ¼ cup water
2 tablespoons minced red onion	2 to 3 tablespoons sesame butter
3 tablespoons minced parsley	¼ cup chopped nutmeats
1 carrot, shredded	

Mix all ingredients together up to the currants. Place in a colander lined with cheesecloth and set in the sink to drain. Let sit for 1 hour. Rinse with cold water and then, taking up the sides of the cheesecloth, make a bag and squeeze out excess liquid.

Drain currants and blend cooking water with the sesame butter. Beat together until well blended. Toss all ingredients together in a salad bowl and add dressing.

Beet and Watercress Salad

5 servings

1 bunch beets, including tops	few pinches of salt
1 bunch fresh watercress	¼ teaspoon dill seeds
1 teaspoon oil	

Cut beet tops into 1-inch pieces, discarding hard parts of the stem. Slice beet roots into circles, then stack and cut into matchstick pieces. Chop watercress into small pieces.

Sauté beet roots in oil for 5 minutes. Cover and continue cooking over low heat for 10 minutes. Meanwhile, boil beet tops in ½ inch of water in a saucepan for a few minutes, stirring constantly. Add watercress, a pinch of salt, and boil another 3 to 4 minutes, stirring constantly again. Remove from heat and drain.

116 SALADS

Add a pinch of salt and the dill seeds to the beet roots and cook another 10 minutes. Place cooked greens on a platter and spoon roots on top. If desired, sprinkle with sesame seeds or season with umeboshi juice (see section on beverages for making juice).

Greek Salad
8 servings

1 head romaine lettuce
1 head Boston lettuce
several leaves fresh spinach or Swiss chard
1 red onion, cut into thin slices
½ cup black olives
1 small can anchovies, drained and rinsed in cold water *or* few tablespoons chirimen iriko (tiny dried fish)
3 umeboshi salt plums
2 tablespoons olive oil
fresh parsley, oregano, ⅛ pound feta cheese (optional)

Cut greens into strips 1 inch wide, place in a bowl with onion slices, olives, and fish. If using chirimen iriko, boil for a few minutes in ¼ cup water. Shred plums and rub into vegetables. Cover with plate and weight down with a heavy rock. Let sit for 1 hour.

Toss with remaining ingredients and serve. If desired, lemon may be used as a flavoring agent in place of salted plums: use 2 teaspoons of salt instead of plums during pressing and add the juice of 1 lemon when adding other ingredients.

Salad with Noodles and Corn
5 to 6 servings

1 head iceberg lettuce
4 scallions
½ bunch red radishes
2 teaspoons salt
½ pound noodles, cooked
1 cup cooked sweet corn
umeboshi juice

Quarter lettuce and shred into pieces; mince the scallions and thinly slice the radishes. If possible, use the greens and cut them into ½-inch pieces. Toss all vegetables in a salad bowl with the salt; let stand a minute, then, using your hands, squeeze out all the excess liquid. Place ingredients in a strainer and run under cold water to remove excess salt. Squeeze vegetables again.

Toss noodles, corn, and vegetables in salad bowl, season with umeboshi juice.

VARIATIONS: This is just one method of preparing a quick salad. The salt helps to yang-ize the vegetables. Try various combinations of other vegetables. Grains or cooked beans can be used in place of the corn and noodles.

For a quick boiled salad: boil ¼ inch of water in a pan and add the scallion, stir constantly so water continues to boil, and add the radishes and lettuce and ½ teaspoon salt. Stir constantly over a high flame for 4 minutes, then mix with remaining ingredients.

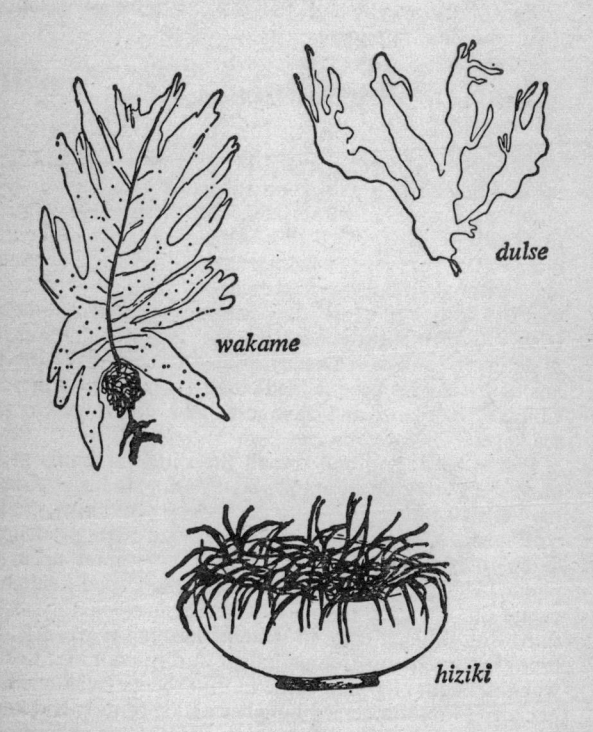

wakame

dulse

hiziki

The Sea Vegetables

SEAWEED can be eaten every day of the year. It is very rich in minerals as well as a good source of proteins, enzymes, vitamins, and carbohydrates. Seaweed will help keep the hair thick and healthy as well as being good for the nervous system. Aside from kelp, most varieties of seaweed (or marine algae) remain unknown to the general public today, but this was not always the case. Our European ancestors imported Irish moss; in North America the Iroquois Indians used dried laver (purple seaweed) instead of salt, while the Indians of the Andes used it medicinally to prevent goiter. The Chinese, Koreans, and Japanese have continued to relish sea vegetables for centuries.

Please be daring and try all the different kinds at least once. You may be hesitant about eating them at first, but they are all rather simple to cook once you know the basic methods of preparation, and they are surprisingly delicious.

There is as much variety in sea vegetables as in land plants. The most common varieties of seaweed available to us are dulse, a deep red variety; hiziki, identified by its long, thin, almost black-colored strands; kombu, a green leathery type that swells up tremendously during cooking; nori and wakame, both of which come in thin sheets (wakame is also packaged in unprocessed bunches and sprouts), and kanten, or agar-agar, used mainly as a thickening agent in desserts. The area where the seaweed grows, the temperature and strength of the current, and other environmental influences all affect its quality and taste. Except for dulse, at present all other varieties of seaweed are imported from the East. However, be wary of inexpensive brands and try to obtain seaweed only through macrobiotic sources as they carry the best grades.

Dulse

3 to 4 servings

1 small package dulse seaweed
several cups cold water
1 teaspoon oil
1 or 2 small onions, thinly sliced (optional)

Rinse dulse briefly in a strainer with cold running water. Look through the leaves carefully, checking for seashells or bits of foreign matter. Place in a deep bowl and cover with enough water so that the dulse is completely submerged.

Soak 15 minutes; then squeeze out excess water and place dulse on a cutting board and chop into 1-inch pieces.

Heat oil in a skillet, add seaweed, and sauté over a high flame for just a few minutes. If using an onion, sauté with the dulse for 5 minutes.

Pour the soaking water over the seaweed, leaving a small amount of water in the bowl. Sand and other matter will sink down to the bottom, so discard this part of the water. Bring vegetables to a boil, reduce flame and let simmer over a low flame; cover with a lid that is left slightly ajar.

Cook 25 minutes or more, until the water has almost completely evaporated.

Hiziki

Follow the same directions for preparing dulse, but unless the strands are very long, hiziki need not be cut. Add a few tablespoons of tamari near the end of cooking. For variety, try making hiziki with roasted sesame seeds, or carrots, lotus root, or burdock.

Cooked hiziki is delicious in salads, with fried rice, or used as a stuffing in knishes or rice balls. Hiziki tastes even better when reheated the next day, and keeps several days in the refrigerator.

Kombu

Three common forms of kombu seaweed are dashi, nato, and torro. Dashi kombu comes in thick sheets, nato kombu has been cut into thin slivers and resembles hiziki in appearance. Torro has a powdery appearance and may be added directly to soups and other dishes just before serving, for it needs very little cooking and does not require pre-soaking.

Sautéed Kombu

Wash either nato or dashi kombu quickly in cold water. Soak kombu in enough water to completely submerge it. Or you can use dashi kombu that has been pre-boiled in a soup stock. If using dashi, cut softened pieces into strips 1 inch long and ½ inch wide. If using nato, simply squeeze out excess liquid. Sauté seaweed in 1 teaspoon oil. An onion and a carrot or two, cut into small pieces, may be sautéed with the kombu.

Sauté for 10 minutes. Add the soaking water and cover. Cook for 30 minutes, then season with a tablespoon or two of tamari, and continue cooking for another 10 or 15 minutes.

Wakame

Wakame may be prepared in the same way as dulse. Wakame sprouts are also quite good; after soaking sprouts, cut out the tough center stem before cooking. The following recipe is for faster cooking; this method is recommended for summer.

Wakame and Onion

4 to 5 servings

½ package wakame (about 1½ to 1¾ ounces)
2 onions, chopped
2 or 3 umeboshi plums, shredded
several cups of water for soaking

Wash wakame and soak for 10 to 15 minutes. Strain wakame and set aside. Pour soaking water in a saucepan and bring to a boil. Add onions and simmer for a few minutes.

Chop wakame into small pieces and add to boiling onions; cook for 5 more minutes, add shredded plums, and simmer for another 5 minutes.

Seaweed Wrappings for Rice Balls

Rich balls are handy traveling companions—you can prepare them for lunch, picnics, or short trips. They will keep for three or four days without refrigeration, even in hot weather.

For 6 rice balls you will need:

6 sheets of nori or wakame seaweed, *or* 1 small package of torro kombu	solution of 5 percent sea salt and water in a shallow bowl
3 umeboshi salt plums	3 cups freshly cooked rice

Toast the seaweed sheets by waving over an open flame until crisp; if using torro, dry-roast in a cast-iron skillet over a high flame for a few minutes, then pour into a shallow pan. Tear the salt plums in half.

First dip your hands into the water, then taking about ½ cup of rice at a time, compress it into a ball; repeat until you have finished all 6 balls. Press one finger deeply into the rice ball and insert the plum, pressing the ball back together to seal hole.

Moisten your hands again and wrap one sheet of seaweed around each ball. If using torro, moisten rice balls slightly with salt water and roll in seaweed until completely covered.

Rice balls keep best when stored in waxed paper. Do not store in tinfoil or tightly sealed container; otherwise the rice will turn sour very rapidly.

VARIATIONS: Rice balls are delicious when rolled first in sesame salt before being covered with seaweed.

Other ways of preparing nori or wakame depend upon your imagination. Deep-fried laver tastes amazingly like bacon.

	Food Content						Mineral Content in Milligrams						
	Water	Protein	Fat	Carbo-hydrate	Fiber	Ash (Minerals)	Ca	K	Na	Mg	P	Fe	I
Nori	11.1	34.2	0.07	40.5	4.8	8.7	470	—	—	—	580	23	—
Kombu	14.7	7.3	1.1	51.9	3.0	3.0	800	—	2,500	—	150	—	—
Wakame	16.0	12.7	1.5	47.8	3.6	18.4	1,300	—	11	—	260	13	—
Hiziki	16.8	5.6	0.8	29.8	13.0	34.0	1,400	—	—	—	56	30	—
Kanten	20.1	2.3	0.1	74.6	0	2.9	400–500	—	—	—	22	6.3	0.2
Dulse	*	25.3	3.2	44.2	—	26.7	300	8,100	2,100	220	270	150	8

NOTE: Contents are indicated in grams, per 100 grams of seaweed.

— Indicates insufficient information available.

* Moisture content varies.

(Reprinted with permission from the East-West Journal. Data on dulse supplied by Fletcher W. Harvey, Seal Cove, Grand Manan, N.B, Canada.)

Pickles

IT'S EASY to make tasty pickles that are ready to eat in just a few days time. Just about any vegetable may be pickled in a simple brine solution or with salt alone. If you want to preserve pickles, follow directions for canning fruits by the "cold pack method" given in the canning section of any basic cookbook, using the ingredients suggested on the next page. Otherwise, store pickles made in a brine solution in a cool place or refrigerator to prevent further fermentation.

Simple Chinese Cabbage Pickles

For each head of Chinese cabbage use:

1¾ tablespoons sea salt   Japanese salad press *or* bowl and plate with a heavy weight

Wash cabbage. Remove outer leaves and cut off root. Quarter lengthwise and cut into 1-inch pieces. Mix salt into cabbage and place in a salad press or bowl, covering with the plate and weight. Store away from sunlight.

Leave any excess liquid in container; after about 5 days the pickles will be ready.

Miso Pickles

scrubbed root vegetables   keg of hacho or mugi miso

After scrubbing vegetables (carrots, turnips, white onions, etc.), pat dry with a towel and bury deep into the miso.

Turn pickles every two days; some may be ready in a

week, while others may be left for a month, depending upon size of vegetables and strength desired.

Pickled Cucumbers

For each quart container, use:

- 10 small pickling cucumbers *or* 3 to 4 large ones, cut into quarters lengthwise
- 2 tablespoons sea salt
- 1 cup boiling water
- additional water for filling jar
- 1 bell pepper, quartered
- 1 onion, quartered
- 1 clove garlic, 1 bay leaf, or several sprigs fresh dill weed (optional)

Scrub the cucumbers thoroughly. If using regular cucumbers from the supermarket, peeling is a must because the skins are usually coated with wax. Dissolve salt in boiling water. Place all ingredients in a clean glass container and pour over salted water. Fill to the top with additional cool water.

Cover mouth of jar with cheesecloth to keep out dust and place jar in a warm place away from direct sunlight. After a few days a white scum will form; this should be skimmed off.

Test pickles after 3 days. If they are still green inside, let stand for another day or two. Cover jar and refrigerate.

VARIATIONS: Other vegetables to pickle are cauliflower, zucchini, beet roots, whole onions, etc. Watermelon rind can also be pickled.

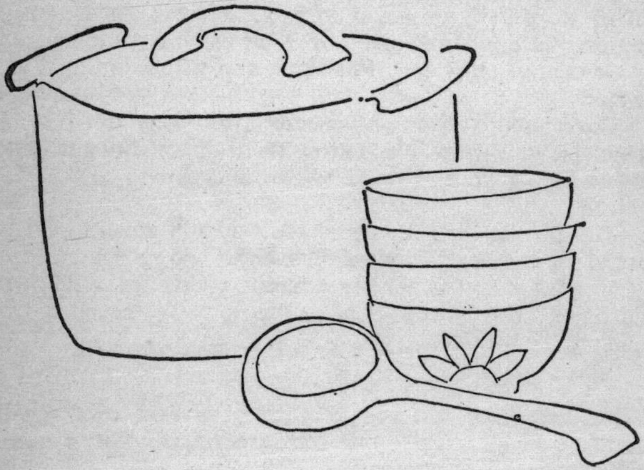

Soups

Clear Stock and Broths

THESE SOUPS can be used with noodles, as a base for cream soups, sauces, in bread, muffin, or pancake batters, or in place of water in cooking vegetables. They add extra taste as well as protein.

Basic Kombu Stock
5 to 6 servings

5 to 6 cups water
1 piece kombu dashi, rinsed in cold water

2 tablespoons bonita fish flakes or chirimen iriko (tiny dried fish)

Boil the water and add kombu; let kombu cook for 5 minutes, then remove. Add fish and simmer for 5 more minutes. Strain again and serve.

Kombu may be reused in a vegetable dish; however, strain out the fish flakes first and feed to the cat. Left in the stock, they will absorb the flavor.

For a clear broth that tastes like bouillon, add ½ teaspoon of salt and 2 tablespoons tamari or miso paste to kombu stock and simmer for a few more minutes.

For a broth with vegetables, add 1 cup sautéed vegetables to stock and simmer for 20 minutes with ½ teaspoon salt. Add 2 tablespoons tamari and simmer for another 5 minutes.

Simple Egg Drop Soup
8 servings

1 piece kombu dashi
8 cups boiling water
1 teaspoon oil
2 onions, thinly sliced
1 large handful dried daikon radish (about an ounce)
3 tablespoons chirimen iriko (tiny dried fish)
¾ teaspoon sea salt
4 tablespoons tamari
1 organic egg
½ cup chopped raw scallions

After rinsing kombu, drop into a soup pot of boiling water and cook for 7 minutes. While kombu is boiling, sauté the onions in a skillet with the oil until they become transparent. Remove kombu from pot, add sautéed onion, daikon, and dried fish and salt. Reduce flame and simmer uncovered for 15 minutes. Then add tamari. Stir egg in a teacup with a chopstick to break up yolk.

Using a pair of long cooking chopsticks, stir soup constantly while slowly pouring egg into soup. Continue stirring for a few minutes until egg is cooked. Serve immediately, garnished with scallions.

The best thing about this soup is that it takes so little time to make and it tastes fabulous! The kombu helps to give it a delicate chickenlike flavor.

Miso Soup

Miso soup is one of the most essential foods of a macrobiotic's diet. In winter we sometimes eat it twice a day, but in summer, because it is so salty, we serve it much less often. Miso paste can be added to just about any soup for flavor, but to enjoy it at its best, try it prepared this way, with just a few vegtables.

Miso Soup
6 servings

1 onion, thinly sliced
¼ head of cabbage, cut into narrow strips
1 large carrot, cut into matchstick pieces
1 teaspoon sesame oil
5 cups water
¼ teaspoon salt
4 tablespoons miso paste

While preparing the vegetables, heat a soup pot and add the oil. Sauté first the onions, then the cabbage and carrots, stirring constantly for about 10 minutes. Add ½ cup of water, bring vegetables to a boil, lower flame, cover and let simmer for 15 minutes.

Add the remaining water and salt and simmer another 10 to 15 minutes. Remove a ladle full of soup stock, add the miso, and mash until the miso is dissolved. Return dissolved miso paste to the pot and stir gently. Cover pot and turn off the flame. Let soup sit for about 5 minutes before serving. The miso should not actually be cooked, merely heated; high heat will kill the valuable enzymes.

For variety, add 2 tablespoons of sesame butter during the last 10 minutes of cooking.

Miso–Wakame Soup

5 to 6 servings

1 teaspoon sesame oil	1 large sheet of wakame *or* 1 handful of dried wakame
1 onion, thinly sliced	
6 cups water	4 tablespoons mugi miso

Heat oil in soup pot and sauté the onion for at least 5 minutes. Add water and bring to a boil. If using sheet wakame, first crumple it with your hands into a strainer, rinse quickly in cold water, and add to soup stock. If using the regular wakame, soak for 10 minutes in about 2 cups of cold water. Squeeze and then chop into pieces before adding to soup. Soaking water should be saved for another dish—it is too salty for this preparation.

Let soup simmer for 20 minutes. Dilute miso in a small amount of stock and add to pot. Turn off heat and wait about 5 minutes before serving, to allow the flavors to blend.

For variation you can add a spoonful or two of dried fish or fish flakes during the last few minutes of cooking.

Barley–Split Pea Soup

6 servings

½ cup whole barley	½ cup greens, chopped (turnip, watercress, or dandelion)
½ pound split peas	
6 cups water	2 carrots, chopped
1 teaspoon oil	¼ teaspoon sea salt
1 onion, chopped	1 bay leaf, or pinch of thyme
	2 to 3 tablespoons tamari

Soak the barley and peas overnight in water. Either pressure-cook for 45 minutes or simmer in a soup pot for 1½ hours.

While the barley and beans are cooking, heat the oil in a skillet and sauté the vegetables in the order listed for 10 minutes.

Add vegetables, salt, and other seasoning to cooked barley–pea stock and simmer for another 30 minutes. Add tamari during last 5 minutes of cooking.

VARIATIONS: Use red or green lentils and eliminate soaking time. Wakame seaweed that has been soaked in water for 10 minutes can be used in place of greens.

Old-Fashioned Vegetable Soup

6 servings

1 teaspoon sesame oil
2 onions, chopped
1 cup chopped greens
1 parsnip, diced
1 carrot, diced
5 cups water
1 to 2 cups leftover cooked whole grains, such as barley, millet, or rice
½ teaspoon salt
2 tablespoons gomasio

Heat oil in a soup pot and sauté the vegetables for 10 minutes. Add water, cooked grain, and salt, and bring to a boil. Lower flame, cover, and simmer for 30 minutes, adding gomasio near the end of cooking.

For a creamy texture, add several tablespoons of sesame butter during the last 10 minutes of cooking. For a thicker stock, dilute 2 tablespoons arrowroot starch in ¼ cup cold water and add during the last 15 minutes.

Country Vegetable Soup

8 servings

2 burdock roots
2 teaspoons oil
2 onions, thinly sliced
1 bunch kale or watercress, chopped
2 carrots, cut into thin pieces on the diagonal
7 cups boiling water
½ cup chickpeas, soaked overnight
½ teaspoon salt
2 tablespoons gomasio

Scrub burdock roots thoroughly, cut into thin slivers, and sauté in 1 teaspoon oil. In another skillet sauté the onions in 1 teaspoon oil until they become transparent, add the kale and carrots, and cook for 10 minutes.

Add the sautéed vegetables and chickpeas to a soup pot

of boiling water; when water returns to a boil reduce flame and cover. Cook for 1½ hours.

Add salt and tamari and cook another 20 minutes.

Fresh Corn Chowder
6 servings

3 ears sweet corn	1 onion, chopped
5 cups boiling water	1 zucchini squash, diced
¼ teaspoon salt	1 carrot, diced
½ cup cornmeal	2 tablespoons tamari
2 teaspoons sesame oil	

Clean corn, removing husks and silk, and place in boiling water with salt. Boil for 3 minutes, then turn off flame and let stand for 10 minutes.

Dry-roast cornmeal in a cast-iron skillet over a high flame for 5 minutes, stirring constantly to prevent burning. Pour into a bowl and set aside. Rinse out skillet and replace on burner; heat the oil and sauté the vegetables for 10 minutes, then reduce flame and cover.

Remove corn from water and place on a cutting board to cool. Add the roasted meal to the cooking water and bring to a boil over a medium flame. Now, holding the corn flat against the cutting board, remove the kernels close to the cob with long, lengthwise strokes.

After cornmeal has come to a boil, cover and simmer for 20 minutes. Add sautéed vegetables, cut corn, and tamari, and simmer for 5 more minutes.

Minestrone—A Potpourri of Flavors
8 servings

2 pieces kombu seaweed	½ cup whole barley
8 cups water	¼ cup beans
2 large onions	½ teaspoon salt
½ pound okra or zucchini squash	2 tablespoons tamari
2 sweet red peppers	¼ teaspoon oregano (optional)
1 carrot	¼ cup chopped parsley
1 tablespoon olive oil	4 ounces whole wheat noodles

Rinse off kombu, place in soup pot with water and bring to a boil. Remove kombu at once with a pair of long chopsticks and place on a dish to cool.

While the kombu is cooking, cut up the vegetables: slice the onions into thin pieces, chop the peppers, slice okra into

14-inch pieces, and dice the carrots. Heat oil in a skillet and sauté the vegetables for 10 minutes.

Add the barley and beans to the stock, cover and simmer for 1 hour. Cut the kombu into thin strips and add to the sautéed vegetables. Cover skillet and cook vegetables over a low flame for 40 minutes.

Add vegetables, salt, tamari, and seasoning to the stock and let simmer at least another half hour. Noodles can be added during last 10 minutes of cooking.

Thick Turnip Soup

5 to 6 servings

1 bunch turnips with greens	⅔ teaspoon salt
1 carrot	1 bunch scallions, chopped, *or*
1 teaspoon oil	1 leek, minced
4 cups water or soup stock	1 tablespoon tamari
4 tablespoons whole wheat flour	1 tablespoon sesame butter

Dice turnips into ½-inch pieces and chop the greens into small pieces. Kale, Swiss chard, or spinach can be substituted for turnip greens. Dice carrot. Heat oil in a skillet and first sauté the greens, then the turnips and carrots for 10 minutes. Cover and cook over a low heat for 30 minutes.

Bring the water or stock to a boil and slowly sprinkle in the flour so that the water never stops boiling. Stirring constantly, simmer for 5 minutes.

Purée the cooked vegetables in a food mill and add to the stock with the salt and chopped scallions. Cook soup for another 15 to 20 minutes, adding tamari and sesame butter near the end of cooking.

Cream Soups

We make our cream soups without the use of dairy products, yet they turn out sumptuous and thick with the addition of vegetables and grains. Flour, flakes of grain, or whole grain combined with sautéed vegetables and slow, gentle cooking will produce a wonderfully textured, flavorful soup.

Any of these soups may be cooked down and served the next day as a sauce for grains, vegetables, or noodles for an instant casserole dish.

Cream of Celery Soup
5 servings

2 onions	5 cups water
10 stalks celery	½ teaspoon sea salt
1 tablespoon sesame oil	pinch of thyme or dill (optional)
⅓ cup oat flakes	

Slice the onions into thin pieces; remove outer strings from celery and then cut stalks in half vertically and finally into pieces ¼ inch thick. Heat oil in a soup pot and sauté the onions until they become transparent. Add celery and sauté until it changes color.

Add the oat flakes and continue stirring until they are well covered with oil and are becoming moist. This takes about 5 minutes. Slowly add the water, stirring constantly. Bring stock to a boil and add salt and other seasonings. Cover and simmer 30 to 40 minutes.

VARIATIONS: Toast a sheet or two of nori seaweed and crumble over soup just before serving. Soup may be also seasoned with tamari. Cooked down to about half its volume, this soup makes a delicate sauce for whitefish, lobster, or crab.

Squash Potage
6 servings

3 pounds butternut or acorn squash	½ cup cold water
1 pound onions	1 teaspoon salt
2 tablespoons oil	½ cup grain flakes
	dash of nutmeg (optional)

Scrub the squash thoroughly. If it is organically grown, don't peel it! First cut in half, scoop out the seeds,* then place on a cutting board and chop into 1-inch cubes. Cut onions in half and slice in thin pieces.

Heat oil in a large skillet and sauté the onions until they become transparent. Add the squash and sauté for 10 more minutes. Cover with ½ cup water, add salt, and bring to a boil. Immediately cover with a tight-fitting lid, lower flame (this creates a seal for the steam), and cook 40 minutes. If pressure cooking, 15 minutes is sufficient time.

---

* If you want to roast the seeds, rinse in cold water to remove membrane, and spread on a dry cookie sheet. Sprinkle with tamari and bake in a slow oven until they begin to pop.

While squash is cooking, toast flakes in a cast-iron skillet for a few minutes over a high flame to bring out their nutty flavor. Bring water to a boil in a soup pot and add flakes. When water returns to the boil, reduce flame and simmer.

Purée vegetables through a food mill and add to flakes. Season with nutmeg and simmer for another 15 minutes.

In cold weather, reduce the amount of salt and add 2 or 3 tablespoons of mugi miso during the last few minutes of cooking time. Roasted pumpkin seeds or chopped raw scallions make an attractive garnish.

VARIATION: Carrots may be substituted for squash.

Cream of Cauliflower Soup
6 servings

2 onions
1 head cauliflower
several leaves cabbage
1 carrot
2 tablespoons sesame oil
6 tablespoons whole wheat pastry flour
½ teaspoon salt
5 cups kombu stock or water
1 to 2 tablespoons tamari

Slice the onions in half, then into thin half moons. First cut out the stem from the cauliflower, then gently break up the head into flowerettes. If there are any outer leaves, cut these into 1-inch pieces. Stack the cabbage leaves and cut down the center rib, then cut each stack into 1-inch pieces. Cut carrot into pieces on the diagonal, then stack and cut into matchstick pieces.

Sauté the onions in 1 tablespoon oil until they become transparent, then add the greens, cauliflower, and carrots. Lower flame and cover for 10 minutes.

While the vegetables are cooking, sauté the flour in 1 tablespoon oil in a small saucepan over an asbestos pad for about 5 minutes.

Add flour to vegetables, then slowly add the stock, stirring constantly. Bring to a boil, add salt, and reduce flame. Cover and simmer for 30 minutes, stirring occasionally to prevent lumping.

Season with tamari and cook another 5 or 10 minutes.

For variety, use chopped watercress or parsley in place of cabbage leaves.

Cream of Miso Soup
8 servings

1 teaspoon oil
2 onions, chopped
3 stalks celery, finely chopped
1 turnip, diced
1 carrot, diced
2 tablespoons sesame oil
10 tablespoons wholewheat or rice flour
5 to 6 cups kombu stock
¼ teaspoon sea salt
3 tablespoons mugi miso

Heat oil in a cast-iron skillet and sauté the vegetables for at least 10 minutes in the order listed above. Then lower flame and cover. In a separate saucepan heat 2 tablespoons oil and add the flour, stirring constantly. After about 5 to 7 minutes, when the flour begins to emit a nutty fragrance and is lightly browned, remove from heat and let cool.

Pour a small amount of the stock into the flour and mix to a smooth paste. Combine with the rest of the stock and pour into a soup pot with the sautéed vegetables and the salt. Bring to a boil over a high flame, then reduce the flame and let simmer with a lid on, for ½ hour, stirring occasionally.

Remove a ladleful of stock and mix with the miso until creamy, then return to the pot. Cook another minute or two over very low heat, stirring gently with a wooden spoon.

For variety, corn, oat, or millet flakes may be used in place of the flour.

aduki beans

pinio beans

black beans

chick peas

Beans

LEGUMES is the general family name applied to pulses, or the edible seeds commonly known to us as peas, beans, and lentils. All are rich in iron, vitamins, and concentrated amounts of protein and starch. The chemical composition of legumes shows them to be similar to animal protein, with a high nitrogen content.

Legumes are more yang than some vegetables, but more yin than grain, and are considered, together with vegetables, as secondary foods. Because of their high concentration of protein and starch, we need only eat them in small amounts, and not every day. However, aduki beans are the most yang of this classification and may be eaten much more frequently than the other varieties.

Black beans, chickpeas, green lentils, split peas, and pinto beans should all be soaked several hours or overnight. For pressure cooking, use about 3 parts water to 1 part beans; for regular cooking use 4 times as much water. Add sea salt or tamari after the beans have cooked, otherwise they will not become tender.

A small piece of kombu seaweed added to the pot will soften soybeans and other more yin beans. Aduki beans should not be cooked with kombu, however, for the natural sodium in the seaweed breaks down their chemical structure and destroys their full nutritional value.

Generally speaking, all beans need to be pressure-cooked about 45 minutes. Season with a pinch of salt after the pressure drops and cook slowly (uncovered) until excess liquid is reduced. For regular cooking bring beans to a boil, reduce to a low flame, and cook 2 to 2½ hours with a cover. Remove lid and follow same directions as for pressure cooking.

Aduki Beans

Beside being the most yang bean, aduki beans are delicious and combine well with many dishes. Try them in desserts, breads and muffins, as well as in soups or cooked with grains.

Aduki Beans and Onions

5 to 6 servings

1½ cups aduki beans	1 teaspoon oil
4 cups water	2 onions, thinly sliced
½ teaspoon salt	

Wash beans in cold water several times. Pressure-cook for 45 minutes. If you are boiling them, use one more cup of water and simmer for 2 hours over low heat.

While the beans are cooking, heat the oil in a small skillet and sauté the onions for 10 minutes and set aside.

After the pressure drops, add salt and sautéed onions. Stirring occasionally, cook beans over a medium flame until they become creamy. Add more liquid if necessary.

VARIATIONS: Baked aduki beans are also very good. Sauté onions and add 2 diced carrots or slivers of burdock root; place beans and vegetables, mixed with 2 tablespoons of miso mashed in a little water, into a casserole dish, cover and bake for 30 to 40 minutes in a 375° oven.

Aduki Loaf

6 servings

½ teaspoon salt	¼ cup minced parsley
2 tablespoons water	1 green pepper, minced
2 cups cooked aduki beans	1 cup cooked macaroni noodles
2 cups cooked kasha	
½ cup toasted oat flakes	1 small onion, cut into rings
¾ cup chopped onions	

Mix salt and water first in a large bowl, and mix in all remaining ingredients except for the noodles and onion rings. Oil a Pyrex bread pan or square baking dish and spoon in half the mixture. Top with a layer of noodles and cover with remaining mixture. Arrange onion rings on the surface.

Bake in a preheated 375° oven for 35 to 45 minutes.

VARIATIONS: Lentils may be substituted for aduki beans. If you want to make "hamburgers," eliminate noodles and beat an egg into the mixture. Form patties by first dipping your hands in water and then pat out on an oiled cookie sheet. Place an onion ring on the top of each patty and bake for only 20 minutes. Makes about 12 patties.

Black Beans

Black beans are very sweet and taste even better the longer they are cooked. Beside being good in soups or cooked with vegetables or rice, they acquire a unique taste when cooked with wheat berries.

Black Beans and Wheat Berries

6 servings

½ cup black beans
2½ cups wheat berries
½ teaspoon salt

Wash wheat berries and beans in cold water and soak at least 8 hours or overnight in 7 cups of water.

If you are in a hurry, dry-roast beans in a cast-iron skillet over a high flame until they begin to pop.

Pressure-cook for 1 hour. For regular cooking, use 8 cups of water and simmer over low heat for 2½ hours in a covered saucepan.

Add salt and simmer uncovered for another 10 minutes, or until excess liquid is driven off.

Sautéed vegetables can be added near the end of cooking for a hearty casserole dish.

Chickpeas

6 servings

2 cups chickpeas
6 cups water
¾ teaspoon salt

Soak chickpeas for several hours or overnight. Either pressure-cook for 1 hour or boil for several hours in a covered saucepan. Add seasoning at the end of cooking.

The variation in chickpea preparation is endless. Mashed

chickpeas resemble potatoes, but are much tastier. For a quick chickpea sauce: Remove about half the cooked chickpeas from the pot and mash or purée. Return to pot, add several spoonfuls of sesame butter and some sautéed vegetables—and voila! A rich, thick sauce. Chopped parsley, chives, or a clove or two of garlic add a pleasant accent.

For chickpea croquettes: Drain chickpeas, mash well, and add ½ cup puréed brown rice, several spoonfuls of minced parsley. Wet hands and roll into small balls. Deep-fry or panfry with a small amount of oil. Makes 24 croquettes.

Red Lentils and Rice

6 servings

½ pound red lentils	1 teaspoon olive or sunflower oil
3½ cups water	½ teaspoon salt
1 onion, chopped	pinch of thyme (optional)
¼ cup chopped parsley	3 cups cooked rice

Wash lentils in cold water several times, then boil in a covered saucepan for 20 minutes. While lentils are cooking, sauté onion and parsley in oil in a small skillet.

Add rice, vegetables, and salt to lentils and simmer uncovered until thick. A tablespoon of tamari or miso can be added for extra taste.

Curried Lentils

6 servings

Follow the above directions, adding ½ teaspoon curry powder and ½ teaspoon ground mustard. Pour lentils over rice instead of mixing them together during cooking.

Mediterranean Style Lentils

6 servings

Sauté a few cloves of minced garlic with the onion and parsley and follow directions for preparing red lentils.

Pinto Bean Stew

5 to 6 servings

½ pound pinto beans, soaked overnight in 3 cups water	2 teaspoons oil
4 burdock roots	3 onions
3 large carrots	½ teaspoon salt
	3 tablespoons miso

Drain pinto beans and pressure-cook with 4 cups water for 1 hour. If you are boiling them, cook for 2 hours in 5½ cups water.

Scrub the burdock roots and cut into thin slivers, or shave with a sharp knife. Cut carrots into pieces on the diagonal, then into matchstick pieces. Sauté the burdock in oil for 10 minutes in a skillet, then add the carrots and sauté for a few more minutes. Cover and cook over a low flame for 40 minutes. Add water if the vegetables appear dry.

Place cooker under cold water to reduce pressure. Bring back to stove, remove lid, and add sautéed vegetables, and simmer over a low flame. Chop onions and add to stew. Add salt and cook for 10 more minutes. Dilute miso in some water or juice from stew, and mix into pot; simmer one more minute and turn off heat. Cover and let stand for 5 minutes before serving.

This is a hearty dish that we often enjoy in cold weather. It is delicious served over rice with crackers and a small serving of salad or sea vegetable.

Bean Casserole

6 to 8 servings

½ pound dry macaroni noodles
2 quarts water
1 cup cooked beans
⅛ cup onions, chopped
½ cup green pepper, chopped
½ cup celery, chopped
1 cup umeboshi juice
3 tablespoons sesame butter

Boil noodles in water for 15 minutes, drain and rinse in cold water. Mix with beans. Place vegetables in a saucepan with umeboshi juice and boil for 4 minutes, stirring constantly. Add sesame butter and blend until creamy; fold into noodles and beans. Serve cool.

Miso

MISO is one of the most versatile foods invented by man. Its unique flavor lends itself well as a base for soups and sauces and spreads, as well as vegetable and fish dishes. Miso also provides a nutritious balance of essential oils, minerals, natural sugars, and proteins and vitamins.

Soybean miso has a long history behind it. Thousands of years ago man discovered the process of fermentation. Wine and beer were two products that grew out of this discovery and so did miso. The combination of time, salt, and vegtable materials transforms miso into a food that is nutritionally superior to its original ingredients.

What Makes Miso So Beneficial?

Traditional Japanese miso is fermented for four days, after which time it is aged for at least one and a half years (except for kome miso which is a younger, less salty miso). The initial ingredients consist of cooked grain, sea salt, cooked soybeans, and water, which are fermented by an enzyme called aspergillus oryzae and then allowed to age. The following is a condensed description of the miso "aging" process which appeared in the September, 1967, and July, 1868, issues of *Health Food Business Review:**

Complex reactions take place during the long aging process,

* The information for this chapter has been reprinted with permission from *The Macrobiotic*, Vol. 9, no. 7.

starches are combined with water (hydrolized) into easily digested sugars, proteins to amino acids, and most of the carbohydrates to organic acids. These organic acids then interact with alcohol formed in the conversion of starches to sugars, and form esters, which, along with some of the amino acids and their salts, account for much of the rare flavor and aroma of miso.

The salt helps to neutralize the excess acidity, while the grain aids in the release and development of enzymes systems which react upon complex carbohydrates and convert them to fermentable sugars.

Barley Miso

Water 51 percent	Fats 4 percent
Proteins 13 percent	Carbohydrates 4 percent
Dextrose 12 percent	Acids 2 percent
Sea salt 12 percent	Cellulose 2 percent

The food that is produced by this process is a totally new, wholesome, and delicious end-product quite different from its original ingredients. Most commercially made soybean pastes contain MSG (monosodium glutamate), some contain potatoes, artificial coloring, or preservatives. They are not to be confused with the traditional, naturally aged products sold in macrobiotic outlets.

We use miso daily in our cooking. If you are just getting into the diet, once a day may be too often to use it, especially in summer when you want to cut down on salt. It's a good idea to add a little oil when using miso since the oil helps to balance the salt.

Below are several suggestions for using miso in cooking. For other miso recipes, see the section on soups and sauces and also the recipe index.

Miso–Vegetable Stew

4 to 6 servings

2 to 3 cups sautéed vegetables   3 tablespoons water or stock
2 to 3 tablespoons mugi miso

Use vegetables that have been cooked for at least 45 to 60 minutes and are very soft. Mix miso with liquid until creamy, and gently stir into vegetables. Continue to cook another 5 minutes over a very low heat. High temperatures kill the valuable enzymes in miso.

Miso–Rice

4 servings

4 cups cooked short-grain brown rice
1 tablespoon sesame butter
2 tablespoons miso
¼ cup water or stock

In a heavy pot heat rice over a slow flame. When rice is hot, blend sesame butter and miso together with liquid until creamy and stir into rice. Cook over a low flame for several minutes to blend flavors.

This preparation may be combined with cooked sautéed vegetables. Miso stew may also be prepared with oats, barley, or rye cereal for a hearty breakfast on cold mornings.

Miso Stew with Vegetables

6 servings

½ teaspoon oil
½ cup diced carrots
½ cup cabbage
3½ cups cooked brown rice
2 cups water
3 tablespoons miso

Heat oil in a soup pot or dutch oven and sauté vegetables over a high flame for 5 minutes. Add rice and water, and cover; simmer for 1 hour. Just before serving, remove some of the liquid and place in a bowl with miso. Mash well and return to pot. Let miso blend into the stew for a few minutes before serving.

For variety, try other combinations of vegetables, such as burdock and celery. This hearty dish can be served for breakfast, lunch, or dinner to 4 hungry people.

Miso–Vegetable Spoon Bread

Here's a good way to use up extra soup in a bread that's almost a meal it itself.

Serves 6 generously

2 cups miso soup*
1½ cups cooked grain (rice, bulgar, millet, or kasha)
2 cups whole wheat flour (or a combination of whole wheat and corn or oat flour)
1 cup cooked vegetables, e.g., squash, carrots, onions, etc.
2 tablespoons corn germ oil plus extra oil for casserole dish

* If you don't have miso soup, use any other soup and add 2 tablespoons miso.

Combine all ingredients, pour into a well-oiled casserole dish, and bake in a 350° oven. After about 50 minutes a firm crust should form.

Bread will be very soft inside. Test with a spoon; if bread is still wet, replace in oven and cook another 15 to 20 minutes.

Variations on this dish are endless. Try using more grain and less flour. If soup has a lot of vegetables in it, use 3 cups of soup and omit extra vegetables. An egg added to the batter will make a lighter bread.

Tofu

Tofu is a soybean curd with a texture similar to soft cow's cheese and a bland flavor. However, it is marvelous to use in many dishes that call for cheese and is not difficult to prepare.

Homemade Tofu

| 1 pound soybeans | 3 tablespoons fresh lemon |
| few yards of cheesecloth | juice |

Soak the soybeans for 24 hours in 4 cups of water, changing the water every 8 hours. Drain and grind the beans in a hand grain mill or electric blender.

Place in a soup pot, add 2 to 3 parts water, and bring to a boil; lower flame and simmer for 1 hour. Pour liquid through several layers of cheesecloth or fine muslin. Gathering the corners of the cloth to form a sack, squeeze the pulp tightly to remove excess liquid. Pour liquid into a clean glass container, add lemon juice, and stir lightly.

Place pulp aside; rinse off the cheesecloth, and cover the tofu with it. For best curdling conditions, find a warm spot (about 80°) and allow tofu to stand for several hours. Test to see if curd is firm; if not, let stand up to 12 hours more. Strain through cheesecloth to remove excess liquid.

Soy tofu keeps several days in a refrigerator, but it tastes best when first made. It can be crumbled and used in salads, with cooked vegetables, in stews, casseroles, or soups, and is also good eaten alone, seasoned with a dash of tamari.

VARIATIONS: For soy cheese, place a layer of cheesecloth over a bowl and pour tofu through, gathering up the corners of the cloth to form a bag. Secure the top with string, and hang bag over the sink to drain. After a few hours, season cheese with a dash of salt and mix well; cheese is ready to be used, or may be placed in a covered container and stored in a refrigerator for 3 to 4 days.

Special Dishes

Vegetable Knishes

Makes 12 knishes

1 recipe for kneaded dough*

Filling:

3 teaspoons oil
2 cups slivered vegetables
2 to 3 cups cooked grain (rice, buckwheat, millet, bulgar, or cornmeal)
tamari for seasoning, or sea salt

Roll out dough to ⅛-inch thickness and cut into rounds 6 inches in diameter. Stack rounds on pastry board until ready to use.

Sauté vegetables in oil in a large skillet for about 10 minutes. Add cooked grain and continue to sauté for another 5 minutes, until grain is well mixed. Season with a few tablespoons of tamari or ½ teaspoon salt.

For each knish, place several spoonfuls of filling in the

* See p. 94.

To make knishes place filling in center and bring up dough.

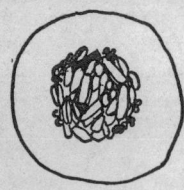

For piroski, place filling off center and make half-circles or

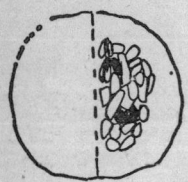

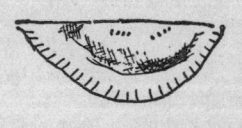

fold over three sides for triangles and pinch edges together.

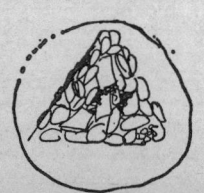

center of each pastry circle and, cupping your hands, bring up the sides of the dough to form a ball. To seal edges together, pinch dough with your fingers. If dough has become dry, use a little water to moisten edges while forming balls. Prick the top once or twice with a fork to allow steam to escape. Place on a lightly oiled cookie sheet and bake 40 minutes in a 375° oven.

VARIATIONS: For a richer, more delicate version, you can make piroski. Use the dessert pie dough,* omitting orange or lemon rind. Cut dough into circles 3 or 4 inches in diameter and place filling on one side of circle. Fold dough over to form a half moon. Seal edges with a fork or use your fingers. Piroski can be made for dessert, using a combination of chopped nuts and fruit as a substitute for the vegetables. Bake for 30 minutes in a 375° oven, or pan-fry for 15 minutes in a cast-iron skillet using a few teaspoons of oil.

Pizza—Macrobiotic Style

Makes 24 three-inch squares

1 recipe for kneaded dough†

Sauce:

- 1 bunch scallions
- 1 tablespoon oil
- 1 cup water
- 4 tablespoons miso

Topping:

- 2 teaspoons olive oil
- 3 large onions, sliced into rings
- ½ pound zucchini, cut into rounds
- 2 green peppers, thinly sliced
- 1 tablespoon chopped parsley
- ½ teaspoon oregano
- ¼ pound tofu or feta cheese, *or* 1 can anchovies

Lightly oil a large cookie sheet and roll out dough directly on top of it. Place in a cool oven and set temperature at 250°. While the dough is baking, prepare the sauce.

Mince the scallions and sauté in oil for 5 minutes. Add water and cover. Let simmer for 10 minutes, then remove a little liquid and dilute the miso with it. Add diluted miso to scallions and simmer over a low heat for a few more minutes.

Heat the olive oil in a skillet and add the vegetables, one

---

* See p. 94.
† See p. 94.

at a time, then sauté for another 5 minutes, adding the oregano while stirring.

Remove the dough from the oven and spread the miso sauce over the entire surface. Arrange the vegetables on top and sprinkle with lightly mashed tofu or cheese. If using anchovies, drain off oil and rinse fish in cold water before garnishing pizza.

Adjust oven to 400° and bake 20 to 30 minutes.

Aduki or Chickpea Pizza

Makes 24 three-inch squares

Mash 2 cups cooked aduki or chickpeas and spread over a dough that has been baked for 10 minutes in a 375° oven. Bake only 15 more minutes. For this one, you can use chopped or thinly sliced onions as a garnish.

Pizza Rolls

Makes 12 to 15 rolls

Form the dough into small 1-inch balls, then roll out into 6-inch circles. Brush each with sauce, then fill with several spoonfuls of vegetables, and a little cheese or fish, fold over sides, and seal with a moistened fork. Bake for 25 minutes in a 375° oven on an oiled cookie sheet.

This is one dish we never try to make quite the same way twice. The fun is in experimenting with different combinations of sauces, vegetables, and toppings. In the fall, cooked and puréed acorn or butternut squash makes an especially good topping. If you are preparing this dish for people not on the diet, you may want to use slivers of tuna, chicken, or pieces of cooked fish (shrimp is super), but the pizza is quite flavorful by itself.

Mexican Chili

8 servings—main course (12 if served as a sauce)

1 pound pinto or kidney beans
2 large onions
3 sweet red peppers
6 stalks celery
¼ cup minced parsley
½ teaspoon sea salt
½ teaspoon oregano (optional)
¼ cup hacho miso (if using mugi, ⅛ cup)

Soak beans for at least 8 hours or overnight in water. Drain and either pressure-cook for 1 hour with 6 cups water or simmer in a covered saucepan for 2 to 2½ hours.

Chop onions, peppers, and celery into ½-inch pieces.

Reduce pressure with cold water. Return pot to stove and remove lid. Be sure to wait until safety valve is completely depressed because beans will continue to cook and are very hot.

Add chopped vegetables, parsley, salt, and oregano, and let simmer uncovered for 20 minutes. Remove a ladle full of liquid from pot and use to dissolve miso; mash in a suribachi or with a wooden spoon until creamy.

Blend in miso just before serving. Chili should have a thick but soupy consistency.

Leftovers taste even better the next day. This is very good in summer with chapatis or corn bread, a fresh salad and, of course, rice.

Chop Suey
6 servings

1 pound burdock root
1 teaspoon sesame oil
3 onions
1 bunch celery or Chinese cabbage
3 ounces wakame seaweed
3 cups cold water

1 tablespoon oil
2 tablespoons arrowroot starch
½ pound fresh tofu or bean sprouts, or slivers of cooked chicken, or shelled shrimp (all optional)
4 tablespoons miso

Scrub the burdock thoroughly with a vegetable brush. Place against cutting board and cut into thin pieces on the diagonal so that each piece is 2 inches long. Heat oil in a small skillet and sauté the burdock for a few minutes, then cover and cook while preparing other vegetables. Burdock takes a long time to cook.

Cut the onions in half lengthwise, then place flat side down on cutting board and cut into thin half-moons. Cut celery or cabbage into strips ½-inch wide. Rinse wakame quickly in cold water; place in a deep bowl and cover with water.

In a large skillet or wok heat the oil, then add the onions and sauté for 5 minutes before adding the celery or cabbage. Squeeze wakame to remove excess liquid. Cut into 1-inch pieces and add to the vegetables; sauté for another 3 minutes. Cover vegetables with water used for soaking, reserving ⅓ cup.

Add the cooked burdock; cover and let simmer several minutes. Dissolve arrowroot in reserved wakame water. Add to pan and bring mixture to a boil.

Special Dishes

If you want to use bean sprouts and/or shrimp, add them to the vegetables at this point; cooked chicken may be added at any time; tofu can be added just before serving.

Remove some liquid from the vegetables and use it to dissolve the miso. Cover vegetables and let them simmer another 10 minutes before adding miso. Turn off heat and let stand for a few minutes before serving.

To serve tofu: Fry cut-up pieces of tofu in a little oil until browned; arrange on top of chop suey and serve directly from wok.

This recipe is delicious served with rice, whole wheat noodles, or another cooked grain such as barley or millet.

Greek Spinach Pie
Serves 6

2 pounds fresh spinach leaves
1 tablespoon olive or sesame oil
⅛ teaspoon salt
½ pound tofu or feta cheese
1 onion, chopped
2 tablespoons minced parsley
1 egg, *or* 2 tablespoons arrowroot starch
1 tablespoon tamari
pie dough for two crusts*

Wash the spinach several times in cold water. Swirl leaves in a large bowl with running water to remove excess sand if spinach is especially gritty. Chop leaves into 1-inch pieces. Heat oil in a skillet and sauté leaves over a high flame for 5 minutes; add salt and reduce flame, cover and let spinach steam for 10 minutes.

Drain and reserve liquid. Mash cheese and spinach together, then blend in onion and parsley. If using arrowroot starch, dissolve with a small amount of spinach juice and then blend into other ingredients. Otherwise, beat in the egg. Add tamari and set filling aside.

Prepare pastry dough according to your favorite recipe, substituting spinach juice for water. Place the bottom layer in a 9-inch pie pan and criss-cross two forks on top of dough. Bake for 10 minutes in a 350° oven. Remove forks and pour filling into crust, cover with second crust, and make several slashes across the top for the steam to escape. Bake another 40 minutes.

* For making pastry dough, see pp. 93–94.

Egg Foo Young
Makes 16 patties

2 cups fresh bean or grain sprouts*
2 to 3 organic eggs
1 cup cooked brown rice
2 tablespoons arrowroot starch
¼ teaspoon salt
2 tablespoons tamari
¼ cup chopped scallions
approximately ¼ cup oil

Sauce:

2 tablespoons arrowroot starch
1 cup water or soup stock
½ cup tamari

Blend ingredients together and mix gently with chopsticks or a wooden spoon so sprouts aren't crushed. Heat oil in a skillet or wok, using 1 tablespoon at a time. When oil is hot, place a large spoonful of batter in the pan. Wait until each patty is set before adding more batter. Allow 10 minutes for each patty.

For sauce: Dilute arrowroot in liquid and mix until smooth. Pour arrowroot and tamari in a saucepan, bring to a boil, and simmer for 10 minutes, or until sauce is very clear and thick.

Serve each patty with a small spoonful of sauce.

VARIATIONS: Cooked greens, such as spinach or kale, can be substituted for sprouts.

Fish

Although some macrobiotic followers tend to prefer a vegetarian diet after a while, fish is one food that is preferred over the other animal products. If you are just getting started with macrobiotics you will probably still crave animal foods and will enjoy having fish several times a week. Later on, you may want to reduce this amount to once a week or less. During the summer we eat very little fish as a rule. Shellfish is not recommended between May and September, for this is their period of reproduction and their bodies contain many toxins.

Most fish is delicious when prepared simply. Fillets of whitefish, salmon steaks, and shrimp can be prepared quickly by first being marinated in a dip made of equal parts of tamari and water with a little grated ginger, and then either

---
* For directions on making sprouts, see pp. 82–83.

pan-fried or broiled with a small amount of oil. To deep-fry fish you can either use a tempura batter or merely dust marinated fish in arrowroot starch and then pan-fry. A mixture of cornmeal and white flour or arrowroot starch will produce a crisper crust.

We generally prepare or serve fish with something yin to help balance it and also to aid in digestion—a small serving of grated white radish seasoned with an equal amount of tamari (similar to horseradish), or a tamari dip made with ginger. A salad or seaweed, sautéed vegetables, and rice complete the meal. More often than not, you'll want a dessert to help balance all that yang; sometimes a small glass of wine is the perfect ending to a fish dinner.

Clam Sauce with Spaghetti
4 servings

- 1 dozen medium-size clams
- 2 tablespoons oil
- 2 minced onions
- 2 cloves garlic, minced
- ¼ cup chopped parsley
- ¼ teaspoon oregano or basil (optional)
- 3 tablespoons tamari
- 1 pound cooked whole wheat or buckwheat noodles

Rinse clams thoroughly in cold water and shell; chop the meat into small pieces and reserve any liquid. Heat the oil and sauté the garlic and onions for 5 minutes; add the parsley and oregano and sauté another minute. Add liquid from clams and cover pan. Let simmer for 5 minutes; add clams and cook another 4 or 5 minutes. Be careful not to overcook clams. Season with tamari and serve over hot noodles.

Fish Chowder
4 to 5 servings

- 1 pound fresh fish (fillets of sole, deep-sea white fish, or scallops)
- sea salt
- 4 tablespoons unbleached white or pastry flour
- 3 tablespoons sesame oil
- 1 onion, chopped
- 1 carrot, diced
- 3 to 4 cups kombu stock or water
- 2 tablespoons tamari
- ¼ cup chopped parsley or scallions

Slice fish into 1-inch pieces (if you are using scallops cut them in half), sprinkle with salt, and set aside. Pan-roast flour for a few minutes in a skillet and pour into a bowl to cool. Rinse out skillet and use it to heat oil, then sauté the onion and carrot for 5 minutes. Add roasted flour and sauté another 5 minutes, stirring constantly. Add stock, bring mixture to a boil, lower flame, and let simmer for 10 minutes. Add fish and cook another 15 minutes, adding tamari near the end of cooking. Garnish with scallions or parsley and serve.

Shrimp Creole
4 servings

- 1 pound unshelled shrimp
- 5 cups boiling water
- 1 piece dashi kombu
- 1 tablespoon sesame oil
- 2 onions, chopped
- 3 sweet red peppers, minced
- ½ pound okra, sliced into ½-inch pieces
- ⅛ teaspoon salt
- 2 tablespoons chopped parsley
- 2 tablespoons tamari
- 4 cups cooked brown rice

Drop shrimp in boiling water, return to the boil, and cook for 5 minutes; strain shrimp and return stock to pot. Rinse kombu, drop in stock, and boil for a few minutes. Remove kombu and save for another time. Shell and devein the shrimp and set aside.

Heat oil in a skillet and sauté the onions, peppers, and okra for 10 minutes. Add sautéed vegetables, salt, parsley, tamari, and rice to stock and simmer over low heat for 30 minutes. Add cooked shrimp and simmer a few more minutes.

VARIATIONS: For a seafood pie, dilute 2 tablespoons arrowroot starch in ½ cup stock. Add to kombu stock and simmer for 10 minutes before adding other ingredients. While stock is cooking, pre-bake a 9-inch pie dough for 10 minutes to a 400° oven. Pour in vegetable–rice mixture and arrange shrimp on top. Cover with a second crust or a thin layer of cornmeal and bake 30 minutes at 375°.

Sole Wrapped in a Blanket
5 to 6 servings

- 1 small knob fresh ginger root
- 2 tablespoons tamari
- 4 tablespoons mu tea, kombu stock, or water
- about 1 pound fillet of sole
- 1 bunch scallions
- 1 cup cooked rice
- 1 package nori seaweed
- 1 teaspoon oil

Peel ginger root and grate finely. Add to the tamari and liquid. Marinate the fillets in this mixture for 20 minutes.

Cut scallions into very fine pieces, and mix with rice. Tear sheets of nori in half and toast over an open flame by waving back and forth until it is crisp.

Place 1 fillet on each sheet of nori with 1 spoonful of the scallion–rice mixture in the center. Roll into a tight bundle. Place the rolled fillets crosswise in a 9x5 baking dish that has been lightly brushed with oil. Bake in a 375° oven for 25 minutes.

If you want to serve a sauce, add leftover marinating liquid to 1 tablespoon arrowroot starch or kuzu dissolved in ½ cup cold water and bring to a boil, stirring constantly. Garnish with chopped parsley or sesame seeds, and serve with the fish.

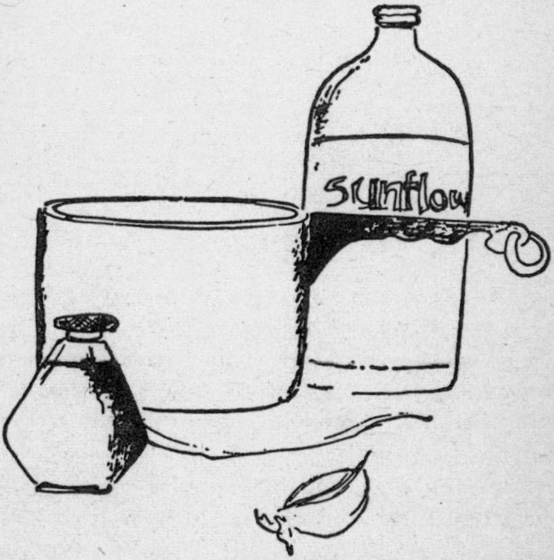
sunflow

Sauces

Béchamel Sauce

For white sauce, use white unbleached flour.
For a light sauce, use whole wheat pastry flour.
For brown sauce, use whole wheat flour.

For each quart of sauce:

⅙ cup sesame oil ½ teaspoon salt
⅔ cup flour 3 tablespoons tamari
5 cups water or soup stock

Heat the oil in a heavy saucepan and sauté the flour, stirring constantly. For white sauce, do this just until the lumps have been dissolved; for a light sauce, sauté until the color is slightly darkened; for a brown sauce continue roasting until the color is rich brown and there is a nutty fragrance (takes about 10 minutes).

Let the pan cool. If you are in a hurry, place pan in a sink and run cold water around the bottom of the pan. Return to stove and slowly add the liquid. Raise flame to medium height and continue stirring until mixture comes to a boil. If there are any lumps, use a wire whisk to beat the sauce. Stir in the salt.

Place an asbestos pad under the pot and simmer uncovered for 20 minutes. Season with tamari and simmer another 5 minutes.

VARIATIONS: Crushed herbs or the juice of several cloves of garlic may be used to accent this delicate sauce. For a summertime dish try using mint tea in place of the water or soup stock.

Onion Sauce Béchamel

Add 1 or 2 finely chopped onions to the sauce when it first comes to a boil and proceed as directed for plain béchamel sauce. A spoonful of sesame butter may be added near the end of cooking for added richness. Other variations: chives, scallions, watercress, or minced parsley.

Miso Béchamel Sauce

Use leftover miso soup in place of some or all of the liquid. For added protein, dilute 1 tablespoon or more of miso with some cooked sauce, blend thoroughly, and add to the saucepan. Turn off heat and let sauce stand for a few minutes before serving.

Miso Gravy
Makes 1 quart

¼ cup oil
⅔ cup whole wheat flour
6 cups water or kombu soup stock
2 onions, chopped
¼ cup minced parsley
½ cup miso paste

Pour the oil into a 2-quart saucepan. When the oil is warmed, add the flour and stir constantly. Cook for 10 minutes, or until the flour becomes nut brown. Remove pan from heat and let cool before slowly adding water. Stir constantly until all the liquid is added.

Return to heat and bring sauce to a boil, then reduce flame and simmer over an asbestos pad for 15 minutes. Add onions and parsley and simmer for at least 30 minutes more.

Blend miso paste with one ladle full of sauce, add to sauce, and continue cooking over a low heat for 5 more minutes.

The secret of this gravy lies in the length of time it is cooked. The longer it is simmered before the miso is added, the darker and richer it becomes. Keeps for 3 days in a refrigerator.

Clear Sauce
Makes about 1 pint

2 cups kombu stock
2 tablespoons arrowroot starch
½ cup cold water
1 onion, minced
¼ teaspoon salt
2 tablespoons tamari
¼ teaspoon fresh grated ginger (optional)

Bring stock to a boil. Dilute arrowroot starch in water and add to stock along with the onion and salt. Let simmer 10 minutes and add tamari and ginger.

This sauce is great when you're in a hurry and goes well with noodles, grains, or fish. For variety use any combination of fresh chopped herbs, or substitute minced shallots or scallions for the onions.

Simple Tahini and Tamari Sauces

For each cup of tahini sauce, use:

4 tablespoons sesame butter
2 tablespoons tamari
12 tablespoons water or clear stock

Place all ingredients in a saucepan and bring to a boil, stirring constantly. Simmer a few minutes until thick.

If you don't want to use so much tahini, try this one:

1 tablespoon arrowroot starch
1 cup water or clear stock
2 tablespoons tahini
2 tablespoons tamari

Dilute starch in liquid. Place in saucepan and bring to a boil. Let simmer 5 minutes, stirring occasionally. Add tahini and tamari and simmer 5 more minutes.

A dash of fresh lemon juice or grated ginger is a pleasant addition in summer.

Tempura Dip

Makes 2 cups

1 knob ginger root
1½ cups strong mu tea or water
½ cup tamari

Peel ginger root and grate finely. If you can't get fresh ginger, use only ½ teaspoon of ginger powder. Mix all ingredients and let flavors blend at least an hour before serving.

To serve, pour a few tablespoons of dip in small saucers or teacups, allowing one for each guest.

For variety, use ¼–½ cup sake or rice wine in place of liquid. Fresh grated lemon or orange rind can be added for extra taste. Minced chives or scallions make an attractive garnish.

Simple Miso Spreads

1 tablespoon miso paste
1 tablespoon water

4 tablespoons sesame butter

Mix ingredients together until creamy. Serve as a spread for bread or crackers. Minced onion or chives can be added as an accent.

Miso–Vegetable Spread

1 cup cooked sautéed vegetables
2 tablespoons miso
1 tablespoon sesame butter

Puree the vegetables in a food mill or mash thoroughly with a fork. Mix in miso and sesame butter and cream together until smooth. Use as a sandwich filling or on crackers.

Miso–Watercress Spread

Makes ½ pint

1 bunch fresh watercress
½ bunch scallions
1 tablespoon sesame oil
3 tablespoons water
2 tablespoons miso

Chop the watercress very finely, mince the scallions, keeping the whites, roots, and greens separate.

Heat oil in a small skillet and sauté first the scallion roots, then the greens and whites, pushing each aside before the next part is added. After a few minutes add the watercress. Sauté for 5 minutes, then add 2 tablespoons of water, cover pan, and simmer for 5 more minutes.

Soften miso in remaining water, add to cooked vegetables, and continue cooking over a low flame for a few minutes.

Serve on grain, bread, or crackers. For a richer spread, add a spoonful or two of sesame butter.

Onion Butter

Makes 1 pint

1 pound white onions
1 tablespoon sesame or sunflower oil
¼ teaspoon salt
1 tablespoon arrowroot starch
½ cup water

Cut the onions in half lengthwise and cut each half into thin half-moons. Heat oil in a skillet and add onions. Sauté for 15 minutes, tossing onions gently. Cover pan and lower flame; cook for 20 minutes. Add salt and cook another 30 minutes. Dilute arrowroot in water. Mash onions with a fork and mix in diluted arrowroot; bring mixture to a boil and simmer for 10 minutes.

This "butter" is extremely sweet and is good as a spread or filling. It will keep for several days in a refrigerator.

Salad Dressings

Cucumber Dressing

Makes 1 cup

1 cucumber
1 cup béchamel sauce
¼ teaspoon dill seeds

Peel cucumber and finely chop or puree in a blender. Mix with béchamel sauce and dill seeds.

VARIATIONS: Use other chopped herbs, such as chives, basil, or mint leaves.

Umeboshi Dressing

Makes about 1½ cups

2 umeboshi salt plums
1 cup water
2 tablespoons minced onion
1 tablespoon minced parsley
1 tablespoon oil

Shred umeboshi plums with fingers and boil with water in a saucepan for 5 minutes. Add remaining ingredients. Simmer for another 2 minutes.

This sauce may be used on salads, vegetables, or fish.

Green Goddess Dressing

Makes 1 pint

2 to 3 umeboshi plums
1 cup water
1 cup cooked soft rice
½ cup parsley, finely chopped
½ cup onion, finely chopped
½ cup watercress or spinach, finely chopped
2 tablespoons sesame or olive oil
1 tablespoon tamari

Shred plums as above and boil in water for 5 minutes. Remove pits. Place rice and juice in a blender set for low speed.

Puree rice for 1 minute, then add vegetables, one at a time until finely blended. Add oil very slowly; blend in tamari. The whole process takes just a few minutes.

Bean Spread

Makes 2½ cups

1 carrot, grated	2 tablespoons tamari
1 green bell pepper, minced	1 tablespoon oil
2 tablespoons chopped parsley	2 cups cooked pinto beans
1 onion, minced	

Put all ingredients except for the beans in a saucepan and cook over low heat for 3 minutes. Puree beans in a food mill, add warmed vegetables, and blend until thoroughly mixed.

Use as a spread on crackers, bread, chapatis, or serve as a dressing on a bed of salad greens.

For variety, substitute black beans, soybeans, or lentils. Two tablespoons of sesame butter may be used in place of the oil. A touch of garlic will also give this a different taste.

Aduki Spread

Makes about 2½ cups

2 cups cooked aduki beans	2 tablespoons sesame salt *or*
1 tablespoon oil	2 tablespoons crushed sesame seeds and ¼ teaspoon salt

Mash beans slightly with a wooden spoon. Heat oil in a skillet and add beans; add sesame salt and sauté for 5 minutes. Serve warm on bread.

Chopped chives or parsley can be added for extra color and taste.

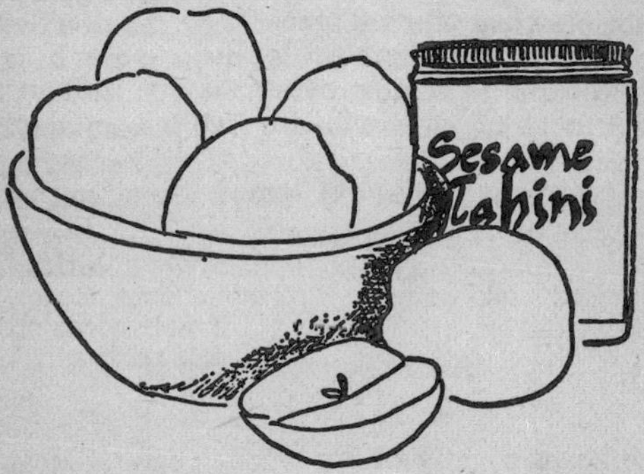
Sesame
Tahini

Desserts

MAKING A DESSERT without sugar, honey, or artificial sweetening agents may sound at first like an extraordinary feat—but once you get the hang of whipping up a satisfying and delicious treat you'll discover that you don't even miss those other ingredients. Natural sugars are brought out through cooking and the use of a little salt.

Most traditional recipes can be prepared with natural sweeteners and a little imagination. Having desserts properly prepared at home lessens the desire to freak out and run to an ice cream or candy store.

Here is a fall dessert that combines two colorful favorites.

Acorn Squash Compote
6 servings

2 acorn squash
1 tablespoon oil
¼ teaspoon salt
3 tart red apples
½ teaspoon cinnamon (optional)
⅛ cup nutmeats

Scrub and peel the squash. Remove seeds and save them for another time. Cut squash into 1-inch chunks and sauté in oil, using a heavy skillet over a high flame. Add a pinch of salt, cover, and lower flame; cook squash for 20 minutes.

If using organic apples do not peel off the skin. Chop apples and add to the squash along with the cinnamon and nuts. Cook for another 30 to 40 minutes, or until the squash is very soft.

166 Desserts

VARIATIONS: All ingredients may be pressure-cooked together with ¼ cup of mu tea. Cook for 10 minutes with medium pressure. To bake: Cut squash in half; scoop out seeds, dust cavity with salt, and fill with chopped apples and nuts. Brush entire surface with oil and bake in a covered casserole for 1 hour in a 375° oven.

Aduki Brownies

Makes 1 dozen 2-inch squares

1 cup aduki beans
3 cups mu tea or water
1 cup chestnut flour or 1 cup pureed chestnuts*
1 cup whole wheat pastry flour
½ cup nutmeats
1 egg (optional)
¼ cup sesame oil
½ teaspoon salt
1 teaspoon pure vanilla extract *or* ¼ teaspoon vanilla powder

Pressure-cook the beans for 1 hour. For regular cooking, simmer in a covered saucepan for 2 hours. Puree the cooked beans in a food mill or blender. Mix with remaining ingredients and pour into a cake pan and bake in a 375° oven for 1 hour.

VARIATIONS: Buckwheat flour may be used in place of half or all of the whole wheat flour. Crushed sesame seeds can be used in place of the nuts. For a sweeter dough, use apple juice in place of the mu tea or water.

Aduki Muffins

Makes about 18 large muffins

2 cups cooked aduki beans
½ cup buckwheat flour
½ cup chestnut flour
1 cup whole wheat pastry flour
¼ teaspoon salt
2 tablespoons oil plus oil for muffin tins
2 cups water, mu tea, dandelion coffee, or kohkoh
½ teaspoon cinnamon (optional)

Mash aduki beans and combine with other ingredients. Oil muffin tins and fill half full with batter. Bake 45 minutes in a 350° oven.

For variety, chopped nuts, raisins, or grated apples or cooked squash can be added or substituted for aduki beans.

---

* If using whole dried chestnuts, boil ½ pound in 1 pint of water for 1 hour, or until soft. To cook fresh chestnuts: slash skin and boil for 20 minutes or bake in a 375° oven.

Buckwheat Muffins

Makes 12 muffins

1½ cups buckwheat flour
½ cup whole wheat pastry flour
1 teaspoon salt
1 teaspoon cinnamon

3 cups liquid (tea, grain coffee, etc.)
oil for muffin tins

Mix dry ingredients, add liquid, and stir until thoroughly blended. Pour into oiled muffin tins and bake 40 minutes in a 400° oven.

VARIATIONS: Chopped nuts or fruit can be added to batter. Or, add ½ cup whole cooked grain, such as bulgar, couscous, or sweet brown rice.

Tangy Applesauce

Makes 1 quart

5 pounds apples
1 cup mint tea or water

1 cinnamon stick
⅛ teaspoon salt

Core apples and cut into eighths. If apples are organic, don't peel them! Place all ingredients in a heavy pot, cover, and cook 20 to 30 minutes.

Put apples through a food mill or sieve to remove skins.

VARIATIONS: Add ½ cup raisins and 1 stick kanten, and cook for another 20 minutes. This makes a very thick, sweet sauce.

Apple–Cranberry Sauce

Makes 1 quart

1 pound fresh cranberries
1 cup apple cider
1 teaspoon cinnamon
½ teaspoon ginger

¼ teaspoon salt
½ cup raisins or currants
3 pounds apples, cored and sliced

Rinse cranberries several times, sorting out rotten fruit. Place in a heavy saucepan or pressure cooker and boil uncovered for 5 minutes with cider and seasoning. Add fruit and simmer with a cover for 30 minutes or pressure-cook for 10 minutes.

Serve warm or cool.

VARIATIONS: Use as a filling for pies, tarts, or strudel.

168 DESSERTS

Chestnut Cream Pudding (Blancmange)
4 to 6 servings

1 stick kanten
3 cups apple juice or mu tea
¼ teaspoon salt
1 cup chestnut flour*

4 tablespoons sesame butter
1 teaspoon vanilla extract (optional)

Soak kanten in apple juice or tea for 20 minutes. In a 1½-quart saucepan simmer apple-kanten or tea mixture with salt for 10 minutes. Sift in chestnut flour, stirring constantly. Cook over an asbestos pad for 15 minutes. Add sesame butter and vanilla and blend until creamy.

Pudding may be served warm or poured into a mold and chilled.

VARIATIONS: For a parfait, spoon alternate layers of chestnut cream with applesauce or other cooked fruit into tall glasses and chill.

Quick Couscous Pudding
6 servings

3 cups mu tea and apple juice (in any proportion desired)
3 tablespoons sesame butter

⅓ cup currants or raisins
⅛ teaspoon salt
1 cup couscous
⅓ cup chopped almonds

Heat liquid in a saucepan with sesame butter and raisins or currants. Add salt, couscous, and nuts, and bring to a boil. Let simmer 1 minute, turn off heat, and cover immediately. Let pan sit 10 minutes before serving.

Gingerbread
Serves 6 to 8

2 cups oat or wheat flakes
1 tablespoon corn oil
1 pound carrots
1 small knob ginger root
⅔ cup chestnut or sweet rice flour
1 cup whole wheat pastry flour

⅛ teaspoon salt
2 cups mu tea
½ teaspoon nutmeg (optional)
1 tablespoon dry Pero†
¼ cup sesame oil
1 egg (optional)
oil for pan

* If using whole chestnuts, see p. 166n for directions on preparing.
† See Glossary, p. 213.

Pan-roast the oat flakes over a high flame in the corn oil for 5 minutes, stirring constantly. Set aside.

Grate the carrots into a large bowl. Peel the ginger root and grate it on the finest side of the grater. Add remaining ingredients, mixing thoroughly. Fold in the flakes and mix batter a few times. Let batter sit for 30 minutes before pouring into an oiled 9x12-inch cake pan. Bake 45 minutes in a 375° oven.

VARIATIONS: Add ½ cup raisins or currants boiled in a little water. Or try it with ½ cup chopped almonds or ½ cup roasted sunflower seeds. A teaspoon or two of poppyseeds can be used in place of the nutmeg.

For a special treat serve with applesauce. If any is leftover, it will keep for a day or two without refrigeration. Will keep fresh 3 to 4 days if refrigerated.

Indian Corn Pudding
6 servings

- ½ cup raisins
- 3 cups mu tea or water
- ¾ cup white or yellow cornmeal
- ¼ cup soy flour
- 2 tablespoons corn oil
- ½ teaspoon salt
- ½ teaspoon cinnamon
- ½ cup nutmeats
- 3 apples
- 1 egg (optional)

Boil the raisins in liquid for 2 minutes, then turn off flame and let stand. Pan-roast the cornmeal in a dry skillet for 5 minutes over a high flame, stirring constantly.

Pour the cornmeal in a large mixing bowl. Pour raisin liquid through a strainer over the cornmeal and stir quickly to prevent lumping. Beat in remaining dry ingredients.

Grate apples directly into bowl. If they are organic, don't peel them! Stir in raisins.

Pour into a casserole and bake for 1 hour in a 350° oven.

Millet Cake
Serves 6 to 8

- 1½ cups millet flour
- ½ cup currants or raisins
- 2 cups liquid (mu tea, apple juice, or water)
- ½ cup sweet rice flour
- ⅓ cup chestnut flour
- ¼ cup sesame oil
- 4 tablespoons sesame butter
- ½ cup chopped roasted almonds
- ½ teaspoon salt
- ½ teaspoon coriander
- ½ teaspoon oil

Pan-roast the millet flour in a dry skillet over a high flame for 5 minutes, stirring constantly to prevent burning. In a saucepan boil raisins in liquid for 2 minutes and let stand on stove.

Blend remaining ingredients in a large bowl, pour over raisins, and mix well for a few minutes.

Oil a bread pan or 9x5x3½-inch cake pan and bake for 1 hour in a 350° oven.

This batter will also make 24 large cupcakes. Brush oil into pans and fill wells half full; bake for 35 minutes in a 350° oven.

Flourless Oatmeal Cookies
Makes 2 dozen large or 3 dozen medium-sized cookies

- 3 cups oat flakes
- ½ cup currants or raisins
- 1¾ cups liquid (apple juice, mu tea, or water)
- ¼ teaspoon salt
- ½ teaspoon cinnamon, nutmeg, or coriander
- ½ teaspoon vanilla (optional)
- 3 tablespoons oil
- ¼ cup roasted sunflower or sesame seeds

Pan-roast oat flakes in a dry skillet over a high flame for 5 minutes, stirring constantly. Boil raisins in liquid for 2 minutes in a saucepan and let stand.

Place oat flakes in a bowl, add remaining ingredients, reserving 1 teaspoon oil, add raisins and liquid, and mix well. Let batter stand 15 minutes.

Preheat oven to 375° and insert cookie sheet to warm. Remove sheet and brush with reserved oil. Mix batter again and use a wet spoon to drop batter onto sheets.

Christmas Rice Pudding
12 servings

- 2 cups raw sweet rice
- 5 cups water or mu tea
- 1 cinnamon stick
- ¼ teaspoon salt
- 1 cup almonds
- 2 cups water
- ¾ cup chestnut flour *or* ¼ cup soy flour and ½ cup pastry flour
- ½ cup sesame butter
- 1 cup raisins
- 1 teaspoon oil

Wash rice in cold water and pressure-cook with liquid, cinnamon, and salt for 45 minutes; or boil for 1 hour in a covered pan. While rice is cooking, boil almonds in water for a few minutes in a saucepan and let stand for 10 minutes, or until skins are easily slipped off between your fingers. Peel the almonds and place on a cookie sheet in a 350° oven and roast for 10 to 15 minutes. Remove from oven.

Remove cinnamon stick from rice and puree rice in a blender or food mill. Pour pureed rice into a large mixing bowl with remaining ingredients and mix thoroughly.

Oil a 2-quart casserole and pour in pudding mixture. Bake 30 to 40 minutes in a 350° oven.

This pudding turns out like a cake—very thick and rich. It makes a lovely holiday dish and can be chilled and served in slices garnished with slivered almonds.

Pies
Makes a 9-inch pie

Pie dough recipe for 2 crusts*

6 to 8 apples, pears, or peaches
1½ tablespoons arrowroot starch
1 cup mint tea or water
⅛ teaspoon salt
½ teaspoon cinnamon

Prepare dough in advance and bake bottom crust in a 350° oven for 10 minutes. Core and slice fruit into eighths. Peeling is unnecessary if fruit is organically grown. Dilute starch in liquid and place in a 2-quart saucepan. Bring to a boil, stirring constantly, and add salt, cinnamon, and fruit. Cook for 10 minutes, stirring constantly.

Pour fruit mixture into baked crust and cover with second crust. Bake 50 minutes in a 350° oven.

VARIATIONS: If using an oat flake crust, cover top of pie by rubbing dough between your fingers until it crumbles and sprinkle it over pie. For deep-dish pie, oil a casserole and dust lightly with flour. Add fruit filling and cover with oat flake crust.

Apple or Fruit Crisp
6 servings

2 cups oat flakes
½ cup whole wheat flour
½ teaspoon cinnamon
¼ teaspoon salt
¼ cup oil
¼ cup liquid (apple juice, mu tea, mint tea)
5 apples or 3 cups strawberries, blueberries, etc.
½ cut currants (optional)
½ cup chopped nuts

Place all ingredients except fruit in a bowl and rub together with your fingers until crumbly.

* See p. 94.

DESSERTS

Place half the mixture in a casserole or 9x12-inch cake pan. Arrange a layer of sliced fruit and nuts, cover with remaining ingredients, and bake in a 375° oven for 40 minutes.

VARIATIONS: Apricot crisp can be made by simmering ½ pound dried apricots in 1½ cups liquid (try part dry red wine, part mint, or mu tea) for 30 minutes with a pinch of salt. Use in place of fresh fruit.

Squash Pie

Makes 2 9-inch pies

- 4 pounds butternut, acorn, or buttercup squash
- 2 teaspoons sesame oil
- ½ cup apple juice
- ¼ teaspoon salt
- ½ teaspoon cinnamon or coriander
- 1 tablespoon arrowroot starch *or* 1 egg
- 2 pie crusts, baked for 10 minutes

Scrub squash and cut into 1-inch chunks. If organically grown, peeling is unnecessary. Heat oil in a large skillet and sauté squash for 10 minutes. Add apple juice and salt, and cover. Simmer for 40 minutes, or pressure-cook for 10 minutes.

Drain some of the excess cooking liquid from squash and puree squash in a blender or food mill. Mix with cinnamon and arrowroot or egg and pour into crust. Bake 30 minutes.

VARIATIONS: Sauté 2 to 3 sliced onions with the squash for a very delicious and sweet taste. Or try alternate layers of applesauce and cooked squash.

Currant Jam

Makes 1½ pints

- 1 pound dried currants
- 3 cups liquid (tea or water)
- ½ teaspoon salt
- 2 tablespoons arrowroot starch *or* 1 stick kanten

Pressure-cook currants in liquid and salt for 20 minutes over a very low flame after pressure is obtained. Remove from heat and let pressure drop. For regular cooking, add an extra cup of liquid and simmer in a heavy saucepan with a tight-fitting cover for 45 minutes.

Strain currants, reserving liquid. Pour liquid back into saucepan and sprinkle with the arrowroot starch, stirring constantly. If using kanten, let it soak in the liquid for 20 minutes before cooking.

Place over a low heat, and when mixture begins to thicken, place over an asbestos pad. Meanwhile, puree the currants in a Foley food mill. Add the puree plus all the leftover pulp to the pot and continue to cook until the mixture is very thick and difficult to stir (about 10 to 15 minutes).

If you want to can this jam, use hot sterilized jars, fill ⅞ of the way, and seal. Otherwise, allow jam to cool before placing in clean glass jars. Cover and store in refrigerator. Keeps for a week.

You can also use this recipe substituting apricots or prunes for the currants.

Fresh Fruit Gelatin
6 servings

2 cups liquid (mint tea, apple juice, or water)
1 stick kanten
1 pint fresh fruit, sliced or chopped
dash of salt

Soak kanten in liquid for 10 minutes. Bring to a boil, add fruit and salt, and simmer for 15 minutes, or until mixture is very thick. Pour into a mold and chill.

VARIATIONS: Two tablespoons of arrowroot flour or kuzu can be used in place of kanten. First dissolve the arrowroot or kuzu in a little cold water, then mix with liquid and cook with fruit until thick.

For plain gelatin, omit fruit and use a mixture of apple juice and dandelion coffee or tea.

Fruit Sherbet
Makes 6 servings

Follow directions above for making fresh fruit gelatin. Place cooked gelatin in a blender with 2 tablespoons sesame butter and flavor with either ½ teaspoon vanilla or grated lemon rind. Blend on low speed to puree fruit. Pour into trays and freeze.

For watermelon sherbet: Cube and puree enough watermelon to make 4½ cups liquid. Cook liquid with kanten or arrowroot until thick and freeze, or chill until firm. Garnish with fresh sprigs of mint leaves or watercress. This light and refreshing dessert is perfect for summer.

Grated raw vegetables can be used in place of fresh fruit to make a vegetable aspic.

Desserts

Toppings for Pies, Cakes, and Cookies

Sesame Glaze
Makes 1 cup

1 cup apple juice
2 tablespoons water
1 tablespoon kuzu or arrow-root starch

2 tablespoons sesame butter
vanilla or almond extract (optional)

Heat apple juice to boiling point in a small saucepan. Dissolve starch or kuzu in water, add to juice along with sesame butter, and cook until thick. Flavor with a drop or two of extract. Spread over top of cake, pie, cookies, etc.

Apricot Glaze
Makes 3 cups

⅔ pound apricots, finely chopped
3 cups liquid (apple juice, mu tea, mint tea, etc.)

1 stick kanten
⅛ teaspoon salt

Soak apricots in liquid with kanten for 30 minutes. Pour into a pressure cooker, add salt, and cook for 10 minutes, or simmer for 30 minutes in a heavy saucepan. Put through a food mill or whip in a blender.

This makes a very sweet topping that can be used as a filling or as a pudding mixed with chopped nuts and/or a cooked grain. The same directions can be followed, substituting dried apples or prunes for the apricots.

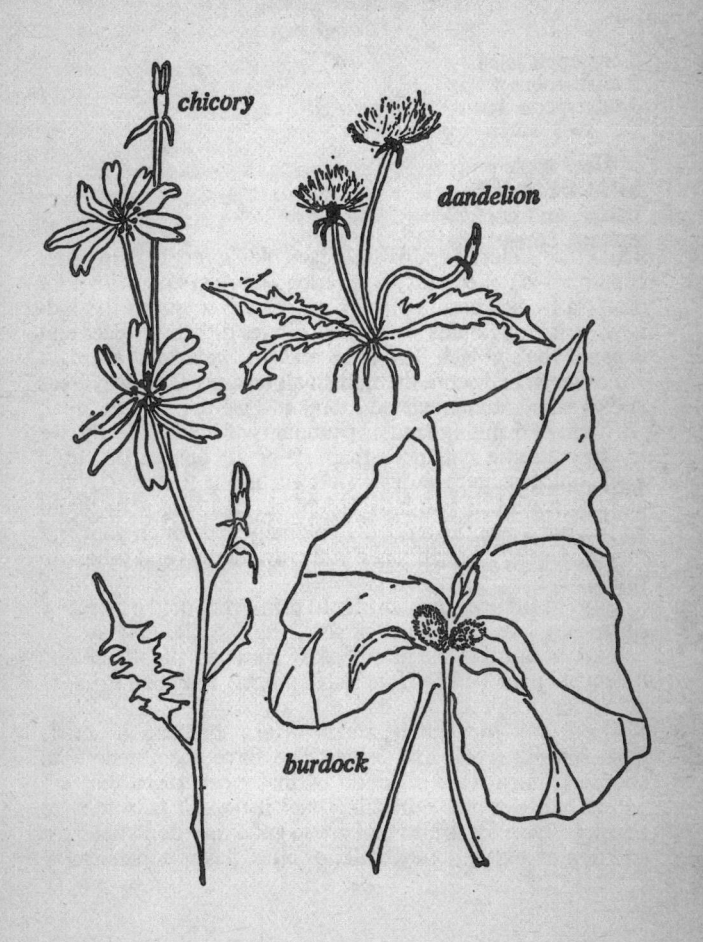

chicory

dandelion

burdock

Beverages

BECAUSE a diet of grains and vegetables is very high in water content, it is unnecessary to overload one's system with a lot of extra liquid. Beside placing an extra burden on the kidneys, drinking liquids with meals dilutes digestive juices and expands the stomach. For these reasons, we drink beverages after meals, and serve them in small teacups. This way, teas and coffees are appreciated more, and we are able to break the habit of drinking excessive amounts of liquid. Ideally, we try to consume not more than 10 or 12 ounces of liquid daily, but this figure varies widely according to our activities and the season. If you have trouble in reducing your liquid intake, cut down the amounts gradually and watch your salt intake. A salty diet will make you crave liquids and other yin foods.

Even in summer, it is unwise to drink very cold beverages, since they have the effect of shocking the digestive system and are harmful to the intestines. In summer, slightly chilled umeboshi juice (made from salted plums) is a good drink to help quench thirst.

There are, fortunately, many drinks that can be made from grains, roots, and leaves. We have the freedom to choose from a wide selection of many beverages that are naturally sweet and refreshing, and it doesn't take long to acquire a taste for drinks that are so good they don't need the addition of sugar, honey, milk, or other flavor enhancers.

Bancha or Kukicha Tea

This green tea comes from the three-year-old growth of leaves near the bottom of the tea bush. It is a pure food, undyed, contains no caffeine, and is not acid-producing. It is our daily beverage, to be sipped slowly after meals in a small teacup. Bancha is the perfect way to end a meal—it is light and very soothing. A wonderful pick-me-up drink can be made by filling a teacup with about a spoonful of tamari and adding hot tea. This drink is called Syo-ban.

To prepare: Dry-roast the tea leaves in a skillet over medium heat until well browned. Shake the pan gently and stir constantly with chopsticks, being careful not to burn the leaves. Just a few minutes cooking is sufficient. Let cool and store in an airtight container. To maintain freshness, roast just enough leaves for a few weeks supply; about an ounce or two is enough.

Simmer about 1 tablespoon of roasted leaves in a quart of water for 10 minutes. The leaves can be reused several times.

In summer, mix an equal amount of bancha and mint tea together. This makes a pleasantly sweet beverage.

Mint Tea

Dried mint teas can be stored in airtight containers and retain their strength for long periods of time. For each serving, use a generous pinch of leaves, add to boiling water, and let simmer about 1 minute. Remove from heat and let leaves steep for a few minutes in the water. If leaves are left to steep too long, the brew may become bitter. Strain and serve. These leaves may be dried and used again.

Grain Coffee

There are several very good varieties of prepared grain coffee available through macrobiotic sources. One is an instant, the others are brewed much the same way ground coffee beans are prepared. However, it is not too much trouble to make your own and it costs about a fraction of the prepared coffees you buy.

Barley Coffee: Wash and drain about 1 cup of *whole* barley. Spread out on a dry cookie sheet and set in a low oven—not more than 250°. Let roast for a couple of hours, stirring occasionally, until all the grains are almost black. This may then be coarsely ground or used whole. Use about 1 teaspoon for each cup of water. Simmer in a coffeepot for 10 minutes. For a slightly bitter taste, add a little roasted chicory root to each pot. Grounds may be used again.

Rye and Barley: Follow the directions above for making barley coffee, using ½ cup rye berries and ½ cup barley. This coffee tastes best when finely ground after roasting. For a sweeter taste, add soybeans that have been soaked overnight and roasted with the grain. Use 1 level teaspoon for each 8 to 10 ounces of water and simmer for 10 minutes. Strain and serve.

Grain Tea

Roast 3 tablespoons of any grain for at least 15 minutes, or until dark brown. Simmer with 1 quart of water for 10 minutes. A pinch of salt may be added during brewing, or season with a few drops of tamari.

Coffees Made from Roots

Different combinations of roasted roots make very delicious full-bodied drinks. Several good combinations are burdock and chicory. Use only 1 part chicory to 10 parts burdock; about 1 teaspoon per cup is usually sufficient. For a strong brew, simmer roots for at least 10 minutes. Dandelion and chicory are another good combination; this drink is also available commercially. For different tastes, try mixing roots and grain coffees together. Or try just one root coffee, such as dandelion, together with bancha tea, and serve slightly cooled in the summer. They are very refreshing.

Lotus Root Tea

Use 1 full teaspoon of lotus root powder for each pint of water. Slowly bring to a boil and add just a few particles of sea salt and a dash of either fresh grated ginger or ginger powder. Let simmer for a few more minutes. This tea forms a sediment at the bottom of the cup so you may prefer to strain the tea while serving. It has a rather chalky texture, faintly similar to cocoa.

Mu Tea

Mu tea is a 16-herb tea that has a strong, fragrant aroma and a spicy taste. However, it is very yang and should not be used too frequently, especially during hot weather. One package makes a quart; simmer for 10 minutes. The little package can be used a second or even a third time. Apple-mu, a good winter party-time drink, is hot mu mixed with an equal part of hot cider. Mu is carried in many health food stores as well as all macrobiotic outlets. It is very good used as a substitute for water in desserts, puddings, and breads, and for an unusual flavor can even be used to make rice.

Burdock Tea

If you want to prepare your own burdock for tea, scrub the roots carefully and then cut into thin slivers on the diagonal, or shave as if you were sharpening a pencil. Place in a cake pan or on a cookie sheet and roast in a 275° oven until pieces are uniformly dark brown. Let cool and store in clean glass containers.

Use about 1 tablespoon of burdock for every 12 ounces of water; bring to a boil and simmer 10 minutes. Burdock is an extremely yang vegetable, and this tea is quite energizing.

Dandelion Coffee

This may be purchased or can be made at home. For homemade coffee: Wash and dry roots. Cut into small pieces and brown in a lightly oiled skillet, using a medium heat. Or oven-roast as for burdock. When roots have cooled, coarsely grind in a food mill or coffee grinder.

Prepare according to the directions for burdock tea. Dandelion roots are also rather yang, and this drink is considered good for the heart.

Umeboshi Juice

1 quart water	2 or 3 umeboshi salt plums

Shred the plums with your fingers and place in a teapot or saucepan with the water. Bring to a boil, then turn down the flame and let simmer gently for about 1 hour. Strain, and add 1 part cold water.

This beverage may be served hot or slightly chilled, and will keep for several days in the refrigerator. It has a unique taste and will help quench your thirst in the summer.

Umeboshi juice can be used like lemon juice as a salad dressing or as a flavoring for vegetables.

Daikon Tea (Dried Radish)

dried daikon   1 pint water

Simmer a small amount of dried daikon in the water for 5 minutes. Strain and serve.

This tea is good for the kidneys; it also acts as a mild diuretic when you want to get rid of excess liquid.

Putting It All Together

> Food when eaten becomes threefold.
> What is coarsest in it becomes feces,
> What is medium becomes flesh,
> and what is subtlest becomes mind.
> —*Upanishad*

UNDERLYING the basic macrobiotic ideas for combining foods at meals is, of course, the concept of yin and yang. In the beginning of the day it is best to start out with foods that are more yin, such as soft cereals, soups, waffles, or pancakes with vegetable spreads and tea. In the evening this pattern is reversed and we prepare foods that are heavier and more yang, such as beans, fish, and fried foods. Thus we can see a balance being created. Night is a more yin time than morning. Thus we eat more yang foods to balance this factor; in addition, we are better able to absorb the more yang foods.

Although modern man is accustomed to eating three or more meals a day, this was not always the case. Many people who are following the macrobiotic way of living prefer to eat just two meals, one in the mid-morning, the other in the evening. However, this depends entirely upon your particular needs and desires. Younger children and pregnant and nursing mothers usually need to eat more often. And many people just beginning macrobiotics may develop huge appetites. However, this tendency tends to diminish after a period of adjustment.

For better digestion and a more refreshing sleep, it is best not to eat or drink immediately before going to bed. By eating at a reasonable dinner hour of six or seven, and retiring around eleven or midnight, we are able to digest food before

182 Putting It All Together

bedtime and our period of sleep will be a time when our organs can relax and replenish themselves. Eating late at night causes our internal system to speed up at a time when all its functions are normally slowing down. This creates unnecessary strain. So even if you're eating the best food, if your eating habits remain chaotic, the foods will not be put to their best advantage.

On the next few pages are some suggested meal-time food combinations. They are intended merely as guides to illustrate the wide variety of possible menu choices.

Suggested Winter Menus

(Numbers on right indicate page of recipe)

I

Breakfast
Whole oat porridge, 75
Whole wheat bread, 90
Miso–vegetable spread, 161
Dandelion coffee, 179

In winter, we try to eat a hot breakfast that will fortify us against the cold. On especially cold mornings, miso soup, or a little miso mixed into grain, supplies an extra protein kick.

Lunch
Pressure-cooked rice, 63
Sautéed carrots and watercress, 101
Hiziki with sesame seeds, 120

Lunch prepared to take to the office or school is a simple affair; foods can be stored in glass jars, with tea or soup in a thermos.

Dinner
Fish chowder, 154
Baked rice, 64
Baked turnips, 108
Applesauce, 167
Bancha tea, 177

If you plan to serve fish, even during winter, it helps to balance it with more yin foods, such as salads, ginger, or desserts.

II

Breakfast
Miso soup, 128–129
Toasted bread, 88
Bancha tea, 177

Unyeasted bread is especially delicious toasted or fried in a skillet with a tiny bit of corn oil and sprinkled with a little sesame salt, or served with a spread.

PUTTING IT ALL TOGETHER

Lunch
Baked wheat flakes, 81–82
Béchamel sauce, 158
Grain coffee, 177

This is a somewhat more elaborate lunch, designed to be served at home; however, occasionally it's nice to fix something special at noon, if you have the time.

Dinner
Buckwheat groats and onion, 71
Black beans, 137
Squash pie, 172
Bancha tea, 177

If you don't have a lot of time to prepare dinner, the pie, rice, and beans can be made in the morning, while the buckwheat groats take just 20 minutes to cook.

III

Breakfast
Buckwheat groats and onion, 71
Rice cream, 64
Bancha tea, 177

Yesterday's dinner leftovers make a fine breakfast or lunch. Or you can cook the cereals the night before if your mornings are rushed.

Lunch
Rice balls in nori, 121–122
Pressed salad, 114–115
Burdock tea, 179

Here is a simple meal that is handy for lunch at work. If you want a more hearty meal, substitute miso or another soup for the tea, and bring along a muffin or some bread.

Dinner
Miso–wakame soup, 129
Millet casserole, 76
Aduki mochi, 67
Roasted chestnuts, 166

What! miso soup again? Yes, and this time teamed up with a very compatible friend, wakame. In our house, it's not unusual to have miso soup twice a day in winter.

IV

Brunch
Wheat cream (See cream cereal, 80
Waffles, 93, with onion butter, 161–162
Grain coffee, 177

On weekends, a brunch of waffles, pancakes, or crepes goes well with a spread, a light soup or cream cereal, and a fragrant cup of grain coffee or tea. You could add sautéed vegetables, salad, or perhaps a light dessert.

Dinner
Rice, 62–63
Chickpea pizza, 150
Crunchy cabbage, 103
Apple-mu, 179

Suggested Summer Menus

I

Breakfast
Cracked rye cereal, 80–81
Chapatis, 91–92
Barley coffee, 178

Summer is a time for lighter meals, and much less salt, animal products, and miso. When making miso soup, use about half the amount of miso you would in winter.

Lunch
Bulgar and onions, 79
Broccoli, 98–99
Aduki brownies, 166

In summer we can take advantage of all the available fresh vegetables, and increase our vegetable intake over the amount we eat in fall and winter.

Dinner
Cream of celery soup, 133
Fried brown rice with vegetables, 65
Summer salad, 115

If you serve a thick or heavy soup, be sure the other foods in the meal harmonize with your selection.

II

Breakfast
Cracked wheat, 80–81
Corn spoon bread, 90
Bancha tea, 177

In warmer weather we can enjoy more often the more yin cereal grains, such as corn, barley, and rye.

Lunch
Rice, 62–63
Vegetable knishes, 147–148
Bancha tea, 177

Knishes make great traveling companions. Like rice balls, they are made with a wrapper and are portable for a picnic or office lunch.

Dinner
Egg drop soup, 128
Red lentils and rice, 140
Wakame and onions, 121
Fresh melon

Although eggs are very yang, the amount of eggs in each serving of egg drop soup is so small that this soup can be enjoyed year round. A little raw fruit is certainly not taboo; try slices of melon sprinkled with sesame salt.

III

Breakfast
Kohkoh (grain milk cereal), 82
Pressure-cooked or steamed carrots, cabbage, or squash
Mu tea, 179

To pressure-cook vegetables, cut in chunks or leave whole, season with a dash of salt or tamari, ¼ cup water, and cook only a few minutes.

Lunch
Couscous, 79
Clear sauce, 159–160
Sweet corn, 74
Mint tea, 177

In summer, you may find rice too heavy to eat at every meal. Couscous is a refreshing change, and so are noodles or other forms of wheat. Mint tea or umeboshi drink can be enjoyed either warm or cool.

Dinner
Rice, 62–63
Tempura of zucchini, 109
Pressed salad, 114–115
Oatmeal cookies, 170

Be sure to serve the tempura with a dip; the dip recipe is on p. 160. In summer, we can eat pressed salad every day if we wish. Raw vegetables help to curb our desire for eating lots of fruit or cold foods during hot weather, and are a better form of yin to balance the effect of a hot summer day.

IV

Breakfast
Boiled wheat flakes, 81
Bread and miso spread, 161
Grain coffee, 177

PUTTING IT ALL TOGETHER

Lunch
Baked brown rice, 64
Greek salad, 116
Barley cakes, 69–70

In summer, boiled rice or baked rice offers a change from pressure-cooked rice. Or try rice cooked with another grain, or beans in the proportion of 1 part grain or beans to 4 parts rice.

Dinner
Rice, 62–63
Egg foo young, 153
Hiziki, 120
Fruit crisp, 171
Bancha tea, 177

The Foods from Yin to Yang

▽▽▽ = very yin
▽▽ = more yin
▽ = yin

△△△ = very yang
△△ = more yang
△ = yang

Cereals
corn ▽
rye
barley
wheat
rice △
millet
buckwheat △△

Vegetables
eggplant ▽▽▽
tomato
sweet potato
potato
Japanese mushroom
pimiento
beans (except aduki)
cucumber
asparagus
spinach
artichoke
bamboo sprouts
mushroom
garlic
green peas ▽▽
celery
purple cabbage
beet
green cabbage
dandelion leaves △
lettuce
endive
kale
turnip
radish
onion
parsley
pumpkin △△
carrot
watercress
dandelion root
burdock

Fish
oyster ▽
clam
octopus
carp
mussels
halibut
lobster
trout
sole
salmon △
shrimp
herring
sardine
red snapper
caviar △△

Dairy Products
yogurt ▽▽▽
sour cream
sweet cream
cream cheese
butter
cow's milk ▽▽
Camembert
Gruyère
Roquefort △
Edam
goat's milk △△

Animal Foods
snail ▽▽
frog
pork
beef
horsemeat
hare
chicken ▽
pigeon △
partridge
duck
turkey
eggs △△
pheasant △△△

Fruits
pineapple ▽▽▽
mango
grapefruit
banana
fig

Fruits (continued)
orange
pear
peach ▽▽
melon
almond
peanut
cashew
hazelnut
olive
cherry
strawberry △
chestnut
apple △△

Beverages
artificially sweetened drinks ▽▽▽
dyed tea
coffee
soda pop
fruit juice
champagne
wine
beer ▽▽
mineral water
carbonated water
water
thyme tea
mugwort △
bancha
chicory
grain coffee
dandelion coffee (strong)
burdock tea
mu tea △△
ginseng △△△

Miscellaneous
sugar ▽▽▽
honey
molasses
margarine
coconut oil ▽▽
peanut oil
olive oil
soya oil
sunflower oil ▽
corn oil
sesame oil
safflower oil

But How Can I Travel and Still Eat This Way?

RECENTLY it has become much simpler to travel and still eat macrobiotically because there are so many new outlets to buy good food, and natural food restaurants keep popping up all over the world.

You'll probably find it best to cook very simply when traveling. If it's just a short trip of a few days, prepare rice balls, salad or sautéed vegetables (pickles are good too), and bake a loaf of bread and cookies or crackers. A jar of spread, such as miso-tahini, roasted nuts or seeds, and toasted nori or wakame are other helpful supplements. Tea can be kept in a thermos or glass jug in warm weather.

If you are camping out, eating can still be uncomplicated. Grains can be washed and lightly roasted in advance, tea leaves and dried seaweed can be put in small envelopes for convenience; small containers of miso, tamari, and oil barely take up any room. Here is a nice trick for making grains when back-packing: place 1 part roasted grain, such as bulgar, buckwheat, couscous, or millet, in a thermos, fill with 2 parts hot water and a pinch of salt, cover tightly and let sit overnight. In the morning you have a fully cooked breakfast ready.

If you plan on a longer trip, and won't be able to use someone's kitchen, take along a small burner, a pressure cooker and a skillet, and a few basic eating utensils and a knife. And if you know you won't be able to get macrobiotic foods, be sure to bring along enough tamari, miso, salt plums, sea salt, and rice to tide you over, supplementing your basics with what's available locally. After all, the idea is to eat what is best suited to your environment, so thinking in terms of yin/yang balance, try to choose foods accordingly.

The listings that follow are designed to help travelers as well as people just getting into the diet who want to know the best place close to them to obtain good foods. Just for the record, did you know that Paris has twice as many macrobiotic restaurants as New York?

Stores and Restaurants in the U.S.

Alaska

Super Natural Foods
3906 Greenland Drive
Anchorage 99501

Arizona

Natural Health Foods
4225 E. Camelbade Rd.
Phoenix 85001

Vitality Health Foods, Inc.
18 S. Central Ave.
Phoenix 85001

Food for Thought
1922 E. Hendrick
Tucson 85702

The Granary
1955 E. Hendrick
Tucson 85702

Arkansas

Old Fashioned Food, Inc.
123 N. 18 St.
Fort Smith 72901

California

Whole Earth Natural Foods
935 G St.
Arcata 95521

The Mustard Seed
Town and Country Shopping Center
Mill Valley & Telegraph Ave.
Berkeley 94704

Osoba Noodle Nook Restaurant
2505 Hearst
Berkeley 94709

Wholly Foods
2999 Shattuck Ave.
Berkeley 94709

The General Store
5th St. between Mission & Junipero
Carmel 93921

The Family Store
Bernadelli Square
Carmel Valley 93924

The Magic Hearth
2 Bernadelli Square
Carmel Valley 93924

Chico San
1262 Humboldt Ave.
Chico 95926

Etidorhpa Natural Foods
114 W. 12th St.
Chico 95926

192 STORES AND RESTAURANTS IN THE U.S.

California (continued)

Spiral Foods
1017 Willow St.
Chico 95926

The Granary
1220 La Plaza
Cotati 94928

Natural Gas Works
1063 Olive Drive
Davis 95616

Escondido Health Foods
405 W. Grand Ave.
Escondido 92025

The Good Earth
123 Bolinas Rd.
Fairfax 94930

Sun and Earth Natural Foods
6576 Trigo Rd.
Goleta 93017

Tao Natural Foods
371 Redondo Ave.
Long Beach 90801

Erewhon Trading Co. of L. A.
8003 Beverly Boulevard
Los Angeles 90048
(wholesale & retail)

Zen Restaurant
5621 Hollywood Blvd.
Los Angeles 90028

Good Morning Natural Foods
242 Commercial St.
Nevada City 95959

Sacramento Real Food Co.
1500 Q St.
Sacramento 95800

Everybody's Natural Foods
1 Saunders Ave.
San Anselmo 94960

Clement Street Natural Foods
522 Clement St.
San Francisco 94118

Far Fetched Foods
1915 Page St.
San Francisco 94117

Hirschfelder Co.
1050 Howard St.
San Francisco 94102

Hunza Natural Foods
728 Vallejo St.
San Francisco 94100

New Age Natural Foods
1326 9th Ave.
San Francisco 94123

Sonoma Natural Foods
3214 Folsom St.
San Francisco 94110

Harmony Food Co.
P. O. Box 1131
Santa Cruz 95060

Natural Foods Store
414 Soquel Ave.
Santa Cruz 95060

Pacific Grain & Grocery
817 Pacific Ave.
Santa Cruz 95060

Rock Island Line Organic
  Food Trip
1915 A Bridgeway
Sausalito 94965

Sonoma Natural Foods
4411 Gravenstein Highway North
Sebastopol 95965

Colorado

Art of Living Co-Op
519 Concord Ave.
Boulder 80301

Green Mountain Granary
1804 14th St.
Boulder 80302

Charles Health Foods
P. O. Box 117
Crested Butte 81224

Living Foods Store
2624 W. 23rd Ave.
Denver 80211

Connecticut

Prospect Mt. Farm
Bantam 06790

Helbing's Delicatessen
Railroad St.
Canaan 06018

Healthwell Natural Food Shop
356 Greenwich Ave.
Greenwich 06830

Horn of Plenty
486 Thames St.
Groton 06340

The Alternative
2614 Boston Post Rd.
Guilford 06437

Cambridge Coffee Tea & Spice House
93 Pratt St.
Hartford 06103

Good Food Store
295 Washington
Hartford 06101

Nature's Harvest
47 Chamberlin Highway
Kensington 06037

Wayne's Health Food Center
Middletown Shopping Center
Middletown 06457

Natural Foods
20 Forrest St.
New Caanan 06840

Fatone Brothers
625 Bank St.
New London 06320

The Fifth Season
165 Bank St.
New London 06320

Healthway Diet Center
60 Broadway
Norwich 06360

White Hart Inn
New England Country Store, Inc.
Salisbury 06068

Not by Bread Alone
Farrell Rd.
Storrs 06268

The Health Food Loft
Box 261, Rt. 83
Talcotville 06066

Evergreen Good Food Co.
499 Danbury Rd.
Wilton 06897

Natural Living Center, Inc.
22 Danbury Rd.
Wilton 06897

District of Columbia

Gazang
3056 M Street N. W.
Washington 20007

Glut Washington Food
2323½ 18th St. N. W.
Washington 20009

Yes
1039 31st St. N. W.
Washington 20007

Florida

Oak Feed Store
2825 Oak Ave. #15
Coconut Grove 33133

Scarborough's Health Food Stores
1441 N. Dixie Highway
Fort Lauderdale 33304

Scarborough's Health Food Stores
623 S. 60th Ave.
K Mart Shopping Center
Hollywood 33022

The Come Together Natural Food Shopper
426 N. E. 65th St.
Miami 33101

Hale's Health Foods
Northside Shopping Center
Miami 33147

Healthful Diet Shoppe
1374 N. E. 163rd St.
North Miami Beach 33162

Feedbag General Store
Box 159, Rt. 4
Pensacola 32504

Perrine Health Foods, Inc.
770 Perrine Ave.
Perrine 33157

Scarborough's Health Food Stores
4028 Bryan Blvd.
Plantation 33314

Tree of Life
% J & L Stores, Inc.
200 Anastasia Blvd.
St. Augustine 32089

Tree of Life
120 6th St. South
St. Petersburg 33733

Sarasota Food Co-Op
1551 Main St.
Sarasota 33578

STORES AND RESTAURANTS IN THE U.S.

Florida (continued)
Second Story Shop
109½ E. College Ave.
Tallahassee 32302

Sun Restaurant
675 W. Jefferson St.
Tallahassee 32302

Georgia

Aquarian Health Food
3340 Peach Tree Rd.
Atlanta 30326

Atlanta Nutrition Center
571 Peach Tree N. E.
Atlanta 30308

Morning Star
1451-53 Oxford Rd.
Atlanta 30301

New Morning Food Co-Op
% General Store
118 10th St. N. E.
Atlanta 30301

The Egg & The Lotus
1782 Cheshire Bridge Rd.
Atlanta 30301

The Good Earth
375 Pharr Rd. N. E.
Atlanta 30305

Ad Infinitum
130 College
Athens 30601

Hawaii

Fourth World General Store
72 Kapiolani St.
Hilo 96720

Good Earth
3520 Waialae Ave.
Honolulu 96813

Illinois

Mr. Natural Food Store
102 E. Jackson St.
Carbondale 62901

Food for Life
2478 N. Lincoln
Chicago 60614

Green Planet Restaurant
2470 N. Lincoln Ave.
Chicago 60614

Hyde Park Health Foods
1360 E. 53rd St.
Chicago 60615

The Growth and Life Store
2937 N. Clark St.
Chicago 60657

Diet House, Inc.
1029 Davis St.
Evanston 60201

Sunrise Farm Stores
17650 Torrence Ave.
Lansing 60438

Indiana

The Clear Moment
116 N. Grant St.
Bloomington 47401

Gerber's Nutrition
111 N. Main St.
Bluffton 46714

Iowa

The Food Trip
2018 College St.
Cedar Falls 50613

The Folks & Uncle Leonard
220 4th St. Tracks
Cedar Rapids 52401

Earth
2225½ University Ave.
Des Moines 50311

Van's Health Foods
Rt. 2
Grinell 50112

Bowery General
518 Bowery St.
Iowa City 52240

Louisiana

Vitality Food Shoppe
4213 Government St.
Baton Rouge 70806

Fine Foods
3236 S. Carrollten Ave.
New Orleans 70118

Shambala
1201 Decatur
New Orleans 70116

Something Beautiful
717 Dante St.
New Orleans 70118

Maine

Seven Seas
West Gate Mall
Bangor 04401

Hunt's Health Foods
56 Weymouth St.
Brunswick 04011

Edward Lyon
395 C. College Ave.
Crono 04473

Feeding Acres Natural Organic Food
Gorham 04038

Port Food Co-Op
Dock Square
Kennebunkport 04046

Axis Natural Foods, Inc.
255 Lisbon St.
Lewiston 04240

Donn's Health Foods
14 Oak St.
Lisbon Falls 04252

Good Day Market
370 Fore St.
Portland 04101

Model Food
113-115 Middle St.
Portland 04111

Root Cellar
246 Main St.
P. O. Box 574
Rockland 04841

The College Bookstore
Div. Springwine Corp.
198 Main St.
Springvale 04083

Natural Foods
105 Water St.
Waterville 04901

Fred Hines Gallery
Rt. 1
Wells 04090

Health Food Store
Middle Street, South
Wiscasset 04578

Maryland

Sun & Earth
1923 3rd St.
Annapolis 21403

Diet & Health Foods
Reistertown Rd. Plaza
Baltimore 21233

Good Earth Organic Grocery
823 N. Charles
Baltimore 21231

Beautiful Day Trading Co.
4915 Berwyn Rd.
College Park 20740

Spring Bottom Natural Foods
53 Bottom Rd.
Hydes 21082

Sundance Brotherhood
9 North Division St.
Ocean City 21842

Kennedy's Natural Foods Inc.
Baltimore Rd. & Rt. 28
Rockville 20851

Massachusetts

Kim Toy Foods
32 Amity St.
Amherst 01002

Laughing Gravey
1 Cook Pl.
Amherst 01002

Whole Wheat Trading Co.
181 N. Pleasant
Amherst 01002

Carl Sauter
Rt. #1
Barre 01005

Stern's National Food Center
261 Cabot Rd.
Beverly 01915

Crane's Call Bakery
112 Queensberry St.
Boston 02109

Erewhon Trading Co.
342 Newbury St.
Boston 02109

Good Food Store
814 Beacon St.
Boston 02109

196 STORES AND RESTAURANTS IN THE U.S.

Massachusetts (continued)
Sanae Restaurants
288 Boylston St.
and
272A Newbury St.
Boston 02109

Life Foods
1349 Commonwealth Ave.
Brighton 02135

Attar
31 Putnam
Cambridge 02139

Corners of the Mouth Restaurant & Store
1419 Cambridge St.
Cambridge 02140

Walden Organic Market
272 Walden St.
Cambridge 02138

Chatham Natural Food Market
587 Main St.
Chatham 02633

Life Naturganic Food Market
480 Main St.
Chatham 02633

American Health Foods
213 W. Plain St.
Cochituate 01778

Concord Spice & Grain
191 Sudbury Rd.
Concord 01742

Yellow Sun Natural Foods Co-Op
P. O. Box 104
Conway 01341

Wendway Natural Foods
P. O. Box 12
Edgartown 02539

Mother Earth
25 Queens Byway
Falmouth 02540

Pure & Simple
37 Elm St.
Fitchburg 01420

Blossom St. Market
143 Blossom St.
Fitchburg 01420

The Life Preserver
280 Worcester Rd.
Framingham 01701

Stern's Farm
859 Edmonds St.
Framingham 01701

The Natural Food Store
Simon's Rock
Great Barrington 02130

Russell's Country Store
94 Central St.
Holliston 01746

Natural Answer
P. O. Box 822
481 Pleasant St.
Holyoke 01040

Nature's Pantry
Main St.
Lakeville Plaza
Lakeville 02346

The Source
50 Central St.
Leominster 01453

Alchemist
96 Main St.
Maynard 01754

House of Natural Foods
100 Main St.
Milford 07157

Mount Toby Trading Post
P. O. Box 156, Star Route
Montague 01351

Natural Food Market
1668 Acushnet Ave.
New Bedford 02740

Natural Health Foods
822 E. Washington
North Attleboro 02760

The Granary
48 Old S. St.
Northampton 01060

Cape Cod Health Food Center
16 West Bay Rd.
Osterville 02655

Natural Foods
47 North St.
Pittsfield 01201

Earth Foods
214 Commercial St.
Provincetown 02657

Stores and Restaurants in the U.S.

Dodge's Cider Mill
Rt. 1
Rowley 01969

Healthway Food Shop
235 Elm St.
Somerville 02143

Mulholland
102 Curtis St.
Somerville 02143

The Health Hut
14 Elm St.
Southbridge 01550

Wellesley Gourmet
27 Grove St.
Wellesley 02181

Like New Health Foods
1274 Washington St.
West Newton 02158

Red Owl
Southampton Rd.
Westfield 01085

Organic Foods
557 Bedford St.
Whitman 02382

Home Sweet Home
Rt. 2
Williamstown 01267

Bread Basket
43 Millbury St.
Worcester 01610

Health and Diet
386 W. J. Boyleston St.
Worcester 01601

Living Earth
327 Pleasant St.
Worcester 01601

Michigan

Eden Organic Food Store
211 S. State St.
Ann Arbor 48108

Vim & Vigor, Inc.
210 S. Woodward
Continental Market
Birmingham 48011

Joyous Revival
1801 S. Woodward
Birmingham 48011

Health Unlimited
5255 Schaefer
Dearborn 48124

Open City Food Co-Op
4551 Third St.
Detroit 48201

Rocky Peanut Co.
2453 Russell St.
Detroit 48207

Family of Man, Inc.
201½ E. Grand River
East Lansing 48823

Sauer's Vita Health Foods
16463 Woodward
Highland Park 48203

Sun Traditional Foods
141 Burr Oak St.
Kalamazoo 49001

Zerbo's Foods
34164 Plymouth Rd.
Livonia 48150

The Carrot Patch
6672 Orchard Lake Rd.
Orchard Lake 48033

Nutri Foods, Inc.
120 S. Main St.
Royal Oak 48067

Minnesota

Carol Natural Foods
811 La Salle
Minneapolis 55414

Shaktih Organic Foods
604 W. 26th St.
Minneapolis 55408

Tao Traditional Foods
3449 Cedar Ave.
Minneapolis 55407

Mississippi

The Granary
3003 N. State St.
Jackson 39206

Zap Boutique
4911 N. State St.
Jackson 39206

Missouri

Chrysalis
8860 Ladue Rd.
St. Louis 63124

Morning Dew
6002 Pershing
St. Louis 63166

New Dawn Natural Foods, Inc.
3175 S. Grand Blvd.
St. Louis 63118

Nevada

Buddy's Health Foods
953 E. Sahara Ave.
Las Vegas 89105

New Hampshire

New England People's Co-Op
Rt. 123 A
Alstead 03602

Galef's Country Store, Inc.
Barrington 03825

Granite State Natural Foods
494 N. State St.
Concord 03301

Fred Reichburger
P. O. Box 325
Derry 03038

Mattapoisett House
P. O. Box 136, Main St.
Dublin 03048

Brookwood Ecology Center
Box 51, Rt. 1
Greenville 03048

Natural Foods
752 N. Main St.
Laconia 03246

The Source
40 Main St.
Lancaster 03584

Honey Gardens
227 Mechanic St.
Lebanon 03766

Earth Things
79 Market St.
Manchester 03105

Nutrition House
1269 Elm St.
Manchester 03101

Uncle Dave's Growing Team
19 Kosciuszko
Manchester 03101

The Old Country Store
Moultonboro 03254

Center of Aquarius Health
  Foods
295 S. Daniel Webster Highway
Nashua 03060

Port O' Call
137 Main St.
Nashua 03060

Living Earth Farm
Rt. #5
Penacook 03301

The Village Store
South Acworth City 03607

Kellerhaus
P. O. Box 356, Rt. 3
Weirs Beach 03246

Do It
52 Main St.
West Lebanon 03784

High Mowing School
Wilton 03086

New Jersey

Natro Health Foods
268 Morris Ave.
Elizabeth 07207

Food for Thought
15 Park Ave.
Madison 07940

Montclair Health Foods
549 Bloomfield Ave.
Montclair 07042

The Health Shoppe
151 Morris St.
Morristown 07960

Back to the Garden Health Food
  Store
43 Paterson St.
New Brunswick 08901

Whole Earth Center of Princeton
173 Nassau St.
Princeton 08540

Third Day
10 Franklin Pl.
Rutherford 07070

Stores and Restaurants in the U.S.

Good Life Health Food Shoppe
Barnstable Court
Saddle River 07458

The Health Food Shoppe
229 Bellevue Ave.
Upper Montclair 07043

New Mexico

The Good Earth Natural Food
Store
P. O. Box 117
Arroyo Seco 87514

Natural Foods
1203 Cerrillos Rd.
Sante Fe 87501

Hummingbird Shop
P. O. Box 1151
Taos 87571

New York

Earth Foods
238 Washington Ave.
Albany 12201

The Store
227 Lark
Albany 12201

Off Center
The Off Campus College's
 Community Store
73 State St.
Binghamton 13902

Nature's Nest
1726 Jerome Ave.
Brooklyn 11235

Allentown Food Co-Op
180 N. Pearl St.
Buffalo 14218

Blacksmith Shop Restaurant
1375 Delaware
Buffalo 14240

New Age Restaurant
457 Grider St.
Buffalo 14240

The Main Street Grainary #1
15 Main St.
Chatham 12037

Potlatch
5 Tompkins
Cortland 13045

Hildegaard's
University Plaza
Eggertsville 14217

Sunrise Health Food Store
148 Canal St.
Ellenville 12428

Tsujimoto
6530 Seneca St.
Elma 14059

Queens Organic Foods
156-05 45th Ave.
Flushing 11355

Farm Store
Rt. #1
Fly Creek 13337

Natural Foods Farm Store
Rt. #1
Fly Creek 13337

Pullman Diet Foods, Inc.
21 N. Franklin St.
Hempstead 11550

Sun Natural Food
7 South 7th St.
Hudson 12534

Korrect Health Foods
Korvette Shopping Center
370-B, Rt. 110
Huntington Station 11746

Ithaca Food Conspiracy
107 S. Aurora
Ithaca 14850

Ithaca Seed Co.
107½ Dryden St.
Ithaca 14850

Belly of the Whale Restaurant &
 Store
271 Floral Ave.
Johnson City 13790

Colonial Health Foods Center,
 Inc.
43 Front St.
Kingston 12401

The Store
Main St.
Margarettville 12455

Movement
350 Broadway
Monticello 12701

200 Stores and Restaurants in the U.S.

New York (continued)
Real Food Store
53 Main St.
New Paltz 12561

Caldron Restaurant & Caldron's Well
308 E. 6th St.
New York 10003

Good Earth
1336 First Ave.
New York 10021

Greenberg's
125 First Ave.
New York 10003

McKay Drug Corp.
301 6th Ave.
New York 10014

Mother Nature & Sons
351 Bleecker St.
New York 10014

Mr. Natural Comes to the City
191 E. Third St.
New York 10009

Nature's Cupboard
80 E. 7th St.
New York 10003

Panacea
323 3rd Ave.
New York 10010

Paradox Restaurant
64 E. 7th St.
New York 10003

Peter Spice
174 First Ave.
New York 10009

Samsari Restaurant
E. 6th St.
New York 10003

Shaping Grain
49 W. 72nd St. #9E
New York 10023

Souen Restaurant
2444 Broadway
New York 10024

Tuvya
325 E. 54th St.
New York 10022

Village Gaslight
116 Macdougal St.
New York 10012

Whole Earth Provisions
156 First Ave.
New York 10009

L & L Health Food Store
Shookville Rd.
Red Hook 12571

Dietary Specialties
1 Cottage St.
Rochester 14608

The Health Food Company
649 Monroe Ave.
Rochester 14603

C. T. Yang
1673 Mount Hope
Rochester 16620

Staff of Life Natural Foods
502 N. James St.
Rome 13440

Never When, Inc.
18 Main St.
Roslyn 11576

Saratoga Traders
16 Caroline St.
Saratoga Springs 12866

Mother Nature's Nutrition
76 Garth Rd.
Scarsdale 10583

Eco-Symbio Co-Op
249 Dunnsville Rd.
Schenectady 12306

The Natural Way
78 Sabonac Rd.
Southampton 11968

State University of N. Y.
Stonybrook Heath Food Co-Op
Rm. 044 Student Union Bldg.
Stonybrook 11790

Juniper Farms
Box 100
Sugarloaf 10981

Brad's Brews, Victuals & Stews
713 S. Crouse Ave.
Syracuse 13210

Central Purchasing Co-Op
459 Westcott St.
Syracuse 13201

Nature's Pantry
122 Trinity Place
Syracuse 13210

Troy Nutritious Foods
451 Fulton St.
Troy 12180

Good Seed
Walkill Ave.
Walkill 12589

Five Rock City Road Restaurant
Woodstock 12498

Sunflower
107 Tinker St.
Woodstock 12498

Woodstock's Health Foods
10 Mill Hill Rd.
Woodstock 12498

North Carolina

The Green Revolution
(N & N Associates)
106 Howard St.
Boone 28607

Harmony
112 Lloyd St.
Carrboro 27515

Earth Inc.
412 W. Franklin St.
Chapel Hill 27514

Wildflower Kitchen
452 W. Franklin St.
Chapel Hill 27514

Sunrise Health Foods
510 Cotanche St.
Greenville 27834

Ohio

Alexander's Health Foods
282 S. Main St.
Akron 44308

Firelands Country Store
Rt. 113
Amherst 44001

Tantic Props Emp.
11½ Mill St.
Athens 45701

Food for Thought
118 W. Woorster
Bowling Green 43402

Eden Natural Foods
347 Ludlow Ave.
Cincinnati 45220

Reality Foods
1126 Carney St.
Cincinnati 45202

Wholesome Earth
2615 Vine St.
Cincinnati 45219

Genesis 1-29
12200 Euclid Ave.
Cleveland 44101

Vitality Health Food Shop, Inc.
51 The Old Arcade
Cleveland 44101

The Food Project
2800 Mayfield Rd. #208
Cleveland Heights 44118

Pluggy's Town Store
P. O. Box 501-2 E. Winter
Delaware 43015

Good Foods Co-Op
Co-Op Bookstore
37 W. College St.
Oberlin 44074

Adam Sigerson
Box 157, Rt. 1
Rutland 45775

Real Good Food Co-Op
Antioch College
Yellow Springs 45387

Oklahoma

L & L Health Foods Company
Box 197, Rt. 1
Fairview 73737

Nutritional Food Center
1024 Classen Blvd.
Oklahoma City 73125

Roger Randolph
1228 E. 29th Pl.
Tulsa 74114

Oregon

Friends of the Earth
41 3rd St.
Ashland 97520

Merrick's Natural Foods
200 N. W. D St.
Grants Pass 97526

Pennsylvania

Pennyfeather
Rt. 2 & 100
Chadds Ford 19317

Natural Health Foods
422 Main St.
Edwardsville 18704

Essene
320 South St.
Philadelphia 19147

Zeitlyn
1025 Westview St.
Philadelphia 19101

Good Earth Natural Foods
2218 Murray Ave.
Pittsburgh 15230

Health House, Inc.
1414 Potomac Ave.
Pittsburg 15216

John McKee Bell's Natural
Foods
5402 Walnut St.
Pittsburgh 15232

New Life Natural Foods Co.
1138 Northway Mall
McKnight Rd.
Pittsburgh 15230

Rhode Island

Alternative Co-Op
78 Biscuit City Rd.
Kingston 02881

The Good Earth
24 Memorial Blvd.
Newport 02840

One Clear Grain
34 Governor
Providence 02904

Walden Center
355 Hope St.
Providence 02904

Cass Ave. Health Center
1025 Cass Ave.
Woonsocket 02895

South Carolina

Sunshine Health Foods
14 B St. Phillips St.
Charleston 29401

Texas

Natural Foods and Country
Store
1911 Ayers
Corpus Christi 78404

Realife Health, Inc.
4441 Lovers Lane
Dallas 75225

Arrowhead Mills
P. O. Box 866
Hereford 79045

Green Acres Organic Foods
1338 Westheimer
Houston 77006

Utah

Word of Wisdom
1007 E. Ninth St.
Salt Lake City 84105

Vermont

Gingerbread Natural Foods
201 Depot St.
Bennington 05201

Spice n' Nice
c/o Country Farm Store
209 N. Bennington Rd.
Bennington 05201

The Good Life
P. O. Box 282
Brattleboro 05301

Guilford Country Store
Rd. 3
Brattleboro 05301

Natural Universe
103 Main St.
Brattleboro 05301

Solanaceae Natural Foods
115 N. Winooski
Burlington 05401

Healy, Inc.
Manchester Depot 05256

McIndoe Farms Inn
P. O. Box 18
McIndoe Falls 05050

Om Natural Health Foods
15 Court St.
Middlebury 05753

Stores and Restaurants in the U.S.

Store Two
2 Park St.
Middlebury 05753

Earth Artisan Co.
RFD #2
Plainfield 15667

Wholemeal
30 College St.
Poultney 05764

Bungaree Natural Foods
RFD #1, Rt. 5
Putney 05346

Butler's Pantry
RFD #1
Putney 05346

Putney General Store
Highway 5 & Kimball Hill
Putney 05346

Zodiac Health Foods
Rt. 5
Putney 05346

Ripton Country Store, Inc.
Box 60, Rt. 125
Ripton 05766

Cold River Farm
21 Center St.
Rutland 05701

Hatch Memorial Library & Store
8 Pine St.
St. Johnsbury 05819

Sunshine Natural Products
63 Eastern Ave.
St. Johnsbury 05819

Old Mill Store
Route 106
South Woodstock 05071

Tweedmeadow Natural Foods
Stockbridge 05772

Warren Store
Warren 05674

Tamarack Farm Mill & Bakery
Weston 05161

Natural Foods, Wee Ski Shop
Main St.
Wilmington 05363

Yankee Clipper
3 E. Eallen St.
Winooski 05404

Virginia

Kennedy's Natural Foods, Inc.
1500 Wilson Blvd.
Arlington 22209

Kennedy's Natural Foods, Inc.
1051 West Broad St.
Falls Church 22046

Store
110 Washington St.
Lexington 24450

Kennedy's Natural Foods, Inc.
6801 Springfield Plaza
Springfield 22150

Washington

Erewhon Trading Co.
3424 N. E. 55th St.
Seattle 98105

Kagetsu Restaurant
45-38 Roosevelt Way
Seattle 98101

Osoba Noodle Nook
1104 N. E. 47th St.
Seattle 98101

Wisconsin

Bay Natural Foods
722 Main St.
Green Bay 54301

Whole Earth Co-Op
817 E. Johnson St.
Madison 53703

Stores, Restaurants, and Centers Outside the United States

Australia

Prana (Store)
398 Milton Rd.
Auchenflower 4066
Brisbane

Belgium

Centre Ignoramus
141 Ave. Voltaire
Brussels

Zen Haus
14 Rue de la Paix
Brussels 5ème

Brazil

Sociedad Macrobiotic (C.I.)
Caixa Postal 1946
Porto Alegre, Rio Grande

Associacao Macrobiotica do
   Estado da Guanabara (C.I.)
Rue do Renzende-21 Apt. 209
Rio de Janeiro G.B.

Canada

Naam Café
2722 West 4th Ave.
Vancouver, B. C.

Golden Lotus
2936 West 4th Ave.
Vancouver, B. C.

Shum Organic Foods
4366 Main St.
Vancouver, B. C.

The Bean Sprout
1709 Barrington St.
Halifax, Nova Scotia

Nu Vite Nutrition Centre
266 King St. East
Hamilton 20, Ontario

Whole Earth Natural Foods
160 McCaul St.
Toronto, Ontario

Zen Food Stores Co., Limited
64 St. Claire Ave. East
Toronto, Ontario

Naturex Inc.
1125 Mt. Royal St. East
Montreal

Pural (retail and wholesale
store)
7494 St. Hubert
Coin Faillon
Montreal

Satori
Claude Painent
Box 54 Station F
1222 St. Urbain
Montreal

Visa-Sante, Inc.
4616 Papineau St.
Montreal

STORES, RESTAURANTS OUTSIDE THE U.S.

Distributors—Sells to stores and official co-ops

Paramount Farms
Sulton, P. Q.

Russel Boyd
Carlsbad Springs, Ontario

Univers. Trading Co.
1192 Queen St. West
Toronto, Ontario

Sunrise Mills
Rt. 2, Preston, Ontario

Denmark

Project House (restaurant)
Radhusstraede, 13
Copenhagen, K

Natural Food Center
Teglgardsstraede, 12
Copenhagen

Helsekost, Gothersgade (store)
Copenhagen

Reformhuset, Rakostdepotet
Skindergade, Copenhagen

France

Paris

Centre Ignoramus, Kameo Store
   & Restaurant, Librairie
   Ohsawa
26 rue Lamartine
Paris 9ème

Aux 4 Céréales (store)
35 rue Nollet
Paris 17ème

The Four Oceans
46 rue des Gravilliers
Paris 6ème

Guen-Mai Restaurant
2 bis rue de l'Abbaye
Paris 6ème

Le Bol en Bois (store and restaurant)
35 rue Pascal
Paris 13ème

Tenryu (store and restaurant)
8 rue Rochebrune
Paris 11ème

Yamato Restaurant
38 rue Nollet
Paris 17ème

Zen Restaurant
40 rue du Faubourg Montmartre
Paris 9ème

Spirale (store)
13 allée de la Fontaine
91 Ste Geneviève de Bois

Outside Paris—Contacts and Activities, Restaurants, and Stores

Alpes Maritimes—06

Mme Pysene, "Le Prieure"
Chemin des Sables
Antibes

Mr. Rosier
3 Place Sainte Marthe
Grasse

"L'Arbre de vie" (shop and cooking preparations)
15 rue Andrioli
Nice

Basses Alpes—04

Mme Billadeau
Village Ecole Mondial
Entrevaux

Bouches du Rhone—13

Zen (store)
Clos Suzanne
Chemin des Infirmeries
Aix-en-Provence

Aux 7 Epis (store)
10 rue des Trois Mages
Marseille (6ème)

Charente Maritime—17

Mme Dufraine
47 bis rue du Perat
Saintes

M and Mme Mornet
217 Avenue du Cimetière
La Rochelle

Deux Sevres—79

Terre Nouvelle (store)
89 rue L. Aguillon
Parthenay

Dordogne—24

Bergerac-Sante (store)
23 rue la Boétie
Bergerac

206 STORES, RESTAURANTS OUTSIDE THE U.S.

France (continued)
Doubs—25

Dr. Bourgeois
86 Grande Rue
Besançon

Haute Garonne—31

M and Mme Guillemaue
 (restaurant)
30 rue Peyrolières
Toulouse

A L'Abondance (store)
1 Place St. Georges
Toulouse

Indre et Loire—37

Centre Regional Ignoramus de
 Touraine
Daniel Guetault
2 rue Fleurie

Loire—42

Au Grain de Blé (store)
77 rue Antoine Durafour
St Etienne

Loire Atlantique—44

Ker Natur (store)
18 Grande Rue
Pouliguen

Morbihan—56

M Rodallec (store)
5 rue Victor Masse
Lorient

Nord—59

Mme Lorthioir (store)
14 rue d'Inkermann
Roubaix

Bas-Rhin—67

Royal Sante (store)
Rue des Serruriers
Strasbourg

Germany

Ohsawa Zentrale
Munsterstrasse 255
Düsseldorf

Holland

Sensei Ohsawa Centre Restaurant
2e Rozendwarstraat 22
Amsterdam

Kosmos Restaurant
Prino Hendrikhade 142
Amsterdam

India

The Cosy Nook
2 Narindar Place
Parliament St.
New Delhi 1

Italy

Centro Dietetico Macrobiotico
 Italiano
Piazza Maddalena 1
Rome

Japan

Tenmi Restaurant
4-3 Sakuragaoka
Shibuya-Ku, Tokyo

Nippon (C.I.)
4-9-1 Nishi-Otiai
Sinjiku, Tokyo

Sensei-Kai (C.I.)
7 Dezima Hamadori
Sakai, Osaka

Portugal

Restaurante A. Colmeia
Rua Da Emenda 11o/2º
Lisbon

Puerto Rico

The Trading Post
101 Calle Degetau
Santurce

Spain

Drugstore (store)
Paseo de Gracia
71 Barcelona

Sweden

Ilse Clausnitzer (C.I.)
Dalstigen, 24
Resaro

Switzerland

Pham Thuc Chuong
1463 Chavannes
Le Chene

J. Rofidal & E. Stadlin
3 Chemin François Lehmann
12, 18 Genève

United Kingdom

Not all of the stores and restaurants listed here are strictly macrobiotic, but they do serve or sell vegetarian foods.

England

Macrobiotic Market Stall
Adam Nicholson
Mother Earth, Stall 3
St. Nichols Market
Bristol

Ceres (store)
269 A. Portobello Rd.
London

Cranks
Marshall St.
London W 1

Cyrano de Bergerac
83 Hampstead
High St.
London NW 3

Good Health
62 Edgeware Rd.
London

Grain
121 Princes Ave.
London

Green Genes Restaurant
8-A All Saints Rd.
London

Manna
4 Erskine Rd.
London, NW 3

Nut House
26 Kingly St.
London, W 1

Raw Deal
65 York St.
London, W 1

Slenders
41 Cathedral
London, EC 4

Slim Inn
16 Maddox St.
London

Harmony Foods (store and distributor)
191 Latimer Rd.
Maidenhead

Scotland

Henderson's
92 Hanover St.
Edinburgh

Vietnam

M. Ngo Thanh Nhan (C.I.)
B. P. 57
Danang

Ton That Hahn (C.I.)
B. P. 22
Saigon

Wholesale Distributors in the U.S.

Arkansas

Shiloh Farms (grains)
Route 59
Sulfur Springs 72768

California

Erewhon Trading Co. (large selection of macrobiotic products)
8003 W. Beverly Blvd.
Los Angeles 90048

Chico San Foods (large selection of macrobiotic products)
1262 Humboldt Ave.
Chico 95926

Massachusetts

Erewhon Trading Co.
33 Farnsworth St.
Boston 02210

New York

Deer Valley Farms (large selection of organic foods)
Guilford 13780

Infinity Food Co.
171 Duane
New York 10013

Mottel Foods
451 Washington
New York 10013

Juniper Farms (organic grains)
Box 100
Sugar Loaf 10981

North Dakota

Pioneer Specialty Foods (grains, nuts, seeds)
Fargo 58100

Pennsylvania

Merit Food Co. (large selection of organic and macrobiotic foods)
Pill Hill Lane
Box 177
Bally 19503

Essene
58th & Grays Ave.
Philadelphia 19143

Macrobiotic Source Books

Cookbooks

Abehsera, Michel, *Cooking for Life*, Binghamton, N. Y.: Swan House, 1971.
———, *Zen Macrobiotic Cooking*, New Hyde Park, N. Y.: University Books, 1968.
Dubawsky, Rebecca, *Cooking with Grains and Vegetables*, Boston, Mass.: Order of the Universe Publications, Box 203, Prudential Center Station, 1968.
Ledbetter, Jim, *Cooking Good Food*, Boston, Mass.: Order of the Universe Publications, Box 203, Prudential Center Station, 1969.
Zen Cookery, Los Angeles, Calif.: Ohsawa Foundation Inc., 1965.

Guidebooks by George Ohsawa

Zen Macrobiotics, Vol. 1, Los Angeles, Calif.: Ohsawa Foundation, Inc., 1965.
The Book of Judgment, Vol. 2, Los Angeles, Calif.: Ohsawa Foundation, Inc., 1966.
The Macrobiotic Guidebook for Living, Los Angeles, Calif.: Ohsawa Foundation, Inc., 1967.
Cancer and the Philosophy of the Far East, Binghamton, N. Y.: Swan House, 1971.
Macrobiotics: An Invitation to Health and Happiness, San Francisco, Calif.: George Ohsawa Macrobiotic Foundation, 1971.

Other Publications

East-West Journal, 20 issues per year, P.O. Box 203, Prudential Center Station, Boston, Mass. 02199.

The Macrobiotic, a monthly magazine, published by George Ohsawa Macrobiotic Foundation, 1471 10th Ave., San Francisco, Calif. 94122.

Makrobiotiskt Nytt (Macrobiotic News), in Swedish, by Ilse Clausnitzer, Vaxholm, Sweden.

The Order of the Universe, a magazine, published by Order of the Universe Publications, Box 203, Prudential Center Station, Boston, Mass. 02199.

Spiral, published in French by Centre Ignoramus de Belgique.

Bibliography

✗ Abrahamson, Emanuel Maurice, M. D., and Pezet, A. W., *Body, Mind and Sugar*, New York: Henry Holt and Company, 1948.

Chase, Alice, M.D., *Nutrition for Health*, Englewood Cliffs, N. J.: Prentice-Hall, 1967.

Composition of Food, U. S. Agricultural Handbook No. 8.

* Davis, Adelle, *Let's Cook It Right*, New York: The New American Library, 1971.

Ford Heritage, *Composition and Facts About Foods*, Woodstown, N. J.: Ford Heritage, 1968.

* Gibbons, Euell, *Stalking the Wild Asparagus*, New York: David McKay, 1966.

Goldstein, J., and Goldman, M. C., eds., *Guide to Organic Food Shopping and Organic Living*, Emmaus, Pa.: Rodale Books, 1970.

Kingsbury, John M., *Seaweeds of Cape Cod and the Islands*, Riverside, Conn.: The Chatham Press, Inc., 1969.

Longgood, William, *The Poisons in Your Food*, New York: Grove Press, 1960.

McCane, Robert Alexander, and Widdowson, Elsie May, *The Chemical Composition of Foods*, New York: Chemical Publishing Co., 1940.

Nicholls, John Ralph, *Aids to Analysis of Food and Drugs*, London: Balliere, Tindall and Cox, 1952.

Ohsawa, George, *The Book of Judgment*, Los Angeles: Ignoramus Press, 1966.

———, *The Philosophy of Oriental Medicine*, Vol. 1, Los Angeles: Ignoramus Press, 1965.

———, *Zen Macrobiotics, The Art of Longevity and Rejuvenation*, Los Angeles: Ignoramus Press, 1967.

Turner, James S., *The Chemical Feast*, New York: Grossman Publishers, 1970.

Yin-Yang, Centre International Ignoramus, 26 rue Lamartine, Paris 9, France.

Glossary

Aduki beans—The Japanese cousin to the American cowpea, a small, hard, red bean with a white dot on the top; the most yang bean—these are eaten more often than any other bean in the macrobiotic diet.

Agar-agar—Also known as kanten, a processed seaweed with gelatinous qualities.

Arrowroot flour starch—A fine white thickening agent prepared from the roots or rhizomes of the Maranta, preferred over corn flour starch for use in cooking. (Corn flour is treated with alkalis and often contains trace amounts of sulfur dioxide due to the sulfite or gas used in its preparation.)

Bancha—The green tea that comes from the three-year-old tea leaves and twigs of the tea bush. High in calcium, it is our daily beverage.

Bonita flakes—Shavings made from dried bonita fish. Used as a flavoring mainly in soup stocks.

Brown rice—Whole, natural rice that has had only the husk removed. Short-grain organic brown rice is the best variety to use.

Buckwheat—Considered a cereal plant, although not a true grain; there are over 150 wild varieties of this plant found in North America alone. More yang than rice or millet, used more often in winter.

Bulgar—A slightly processed form of wheat; used as a cereal or in grain preparations. Has a sweet, nutty flavor.

Burdock—Also known as "gobo," a long, thin root vegetable that grows wild all over North America; used as a vegetable or for tea. Very yang.

Chestnut flour—Made from ground chestnuts; used as a sweetening and thickening agent.

Chirimen iriko—Small dried fish imported from Japan. Used in soup stocks or cooked with vegetables.

214 Glossary

Couscous—A precooked wheat product, imported from the Near East.

Daikon—Japanese white radish. Much stronger than our red radish, it also comes dried.

Dulse—A dark-colored seaweed imported from Canada.

Gomasio—Sesame salt made from crushed roasted sesame seeds and sea salt. Used as a table condiment in place of regular salt.

Hiziki—A black, stringy sea vegetable with a wonderful taste.

Kasha—Another name for buckwheat groats; also used to describe millet.

Kohkoh—A grain milk product; used as a gruel for infants or in desserts.

Kombu—Another sea vegetable. Grows deep in the ocean and has a thick, rubbery texture. Good in soup stocks or as a vegetable.

Kuzu—A vegetable root gelatin. Used medicinally, and also as a thickening agent in sauces or desserts.

Miso—A fermented soybean product used for flavor and protein in many dishes. Buy only the brands carried by macrobiotic outlets. Commercial varieties contain additives.

Mugicha—Barley tea.

Mu tea—A 16-herb beverage with mildly medicinal qualities. Very yang.

Nori—A purple seaweed; comes in thin sheets and only needs to be lightly toasted.

Pero—A coffee substitute made from roasted barley and rye. Found in natural and health food stores.

Sea salt—Unrefined salt made from evaporated sea water. Contains trace minerals.

Sesame butter—Also known as tahini; made from ground sesame seeds. Comes roasted or raw.

Soba—Japanese buckwheat noodles.

Soy sauce—See *tamari*.

Tamari*—A pure soy sauce made during the production of miso. Use only the kinds sold in macrobiotic stores; they contain no additives.

Tempura—Another name for batter-fried foods.

Tofu—Soybean curd. Can be made at home or purchased in Oriental stores.

Udon—A flat, hard wheat noodle. Similar to a heavy spaghetti noodle.

Umeboshi—Salted plums aged in brine for at least 18 months. Used in many preparations with vegetables and salads.

Wakame—A deep green sea vegetable. Combines well with miso for soups and is also delicious with onions.

---

* Tamari is the brand name of a popular soy sauce. Lima soy sauce is another well-known brand.

Index

Aduki beans, 33, 67, 136, 137–38, 213; aduki mochi, 67–68; aduki beans and onions, 138; aduki loaf, 138–39; aduki pizza, 150; aduki spread, 163; aduki brownies, 166; aduki muffins, 166
Agar-agar (kanten), 35, 119, 123, 213
American Indian misickquatash (succotash), 107
Amino acids, 49; chart on essential amino acids, 52
Animal foods, 23, 24, 49, 51, 153; and yin and yang, 187; *see also* Fish; Meat
Apple butter, 35
Apple mu, 179
Applesauce, 167
Apricot glace, 174
Arrowroot starch, 35, 156, 213

Baking equipment, 43
Balanced diet, 21, 45, 46
Bancha (or Kukicha) tea, 33, 177, 213
Barley, 68–70; barley porridge, 68–69; barley with vegetables, 69; barley cakes, 69–70; barley-split pea soup, 129–30; barley miso, 143; barley coffee, 178; barley tea (mugicha), 214

Batters for tempura, 108, 110, 112
Beans, 33, 136–41; aduki beans, 33, 67, 136, 138–39, 213; black beans, 33, 136, 139; chickpeas, 33, 136, 139–40; lentils, 33, 140; storing of, 38; black beans and wheat berries, 78, 139; sprouts made from, 83; pinto beans, 136; cooking of, 137–38; pinto bean stew, 140–41; bean casserole, 141; bean spread, 163
Béchamel sauce, 99, 102, 158–59; onion sauce béchamel, 159; miso béchamel sauce, 159
Beet and watercress salad, 115–16
Beverages, 33, 58, 175–80; bancha tea, 33, 177, 213; diet colas and soft drinks, 58; umeboshi juice, 176, 179–80; mint tea, 177; grain coffee, 177–78; classified according to yin and yang, 188; *see also* Coffee; Teas
Breads, and other things from flour, 56, 86–94; leavened, and unleavened, bread, 56; kneaded dough, 87, 94; unyeasted bread, 88–89; basic doughs for unyeasted bread,

INDEX 217

Breads—(*Continued*)
88–89; rice kayu, 89; whole rice bread, 89; whole wheat bread with millet, 90; corn spoon bread, 90–91; chapatis, 91–92; pancakes, crepes, and waffles, 92–93; crusts and pie dough, 93–94; batters from tempura, 108, 110, 112

Broccoli, 98–99

Brown rice, *see* Rice

Brussels sprouts, 99

Buckwheat, 34, 70–72, 213; buckwheat groats (kasha), 34, 71, 214; buckwheat cream, 71; kasha croquettes, 71–72; kasha spoon bread, 72; homemade buckwheat noodles, 84; buckwheat crepes, 92; buckwheat muffins, 167

Bulgar, 38, 79, 213

Burdock, 99–100, 213; burdock and salted plums, 100; carrots and burdock, 101; burdock tea, 179

Cabbage: crunchy cabbage, 103; simple Chinese cabbage pickles, 124

Caffeine, 54, 58

Cane sugar, 58

Canned and processed foods, 55

Carbohydrates in foods, 26, 53

Carrots, 96, 97, 101–2; cutting of, 96, 97; carrots and burdock, 101; carrots and watercress, 101–2; carrots and sea vegetables, 102

Cauliflower, 102–3; cream of cauliflower soup, 134–35

Cereals: cracked, 38, 80; cream cereals, 80; infant cereal, 82n.; classified according to yin and yang, 187; *see also* Grains

Chapatis, 91–92; basic dough, 91

Chemical flavoring agents and seasonings, 58

Chestnut flour, 87, 213; chestnut cream pudding, 168

Chickpeas, 33, 136, 139–40; chickpea pizza, 150

Chili, Mexican, 150–51

Chirimen iriko (tiny dried fish), 36, 213

Chives, 104, 105

Chocolate, 55

Cholesterol, 55, 61, 62*n.*

Chop suey, 151–52

Coffee, 54; grain coffee, 177–78; barley coffee, 178; rye and barley coffee, 178; made from roots, 178; dandelion coffee, 179

Colas and soft drinks, 58

Condiments, 34–35; storing of, 38, 39

Cookbooks, macrobiotic: list of, 210

Cooked food, storing of, 38

Cooking of foods, 27–31; and macrobiotics, 27–31; why we cook them, 27; use of fire, 28; use of salt, 28–30, 98; time and pressure as yang factors in food preparation, 30–31

Corn, 58, 72–74; corn syrup, 58; making cornmeal with kitchen grain mill, 73; cornmeal for breakfast, 73; corn pancakes, 73–74; baked corn on the cob, 74; boiled corn, 74; pressure-cooked corn, 74; corn spoon bread, 90–91; corn muffins, 91; corn fritters, 91; American Indian misickquatash (succotash),

218 INDEX

107; salad with noodles and corn, 116–17; fresh corn chowder, 131; Indian corn pudding, 169

Couscous, 38, 79, 214; quick couscous pudding, 168

Cow's milk, 55

Crackers, 35

Crepes, buckwheat, 92

Crusts and pie dough: oat flakes crust, 93; whole rice crust, 94; dessert pie dough, 94

Cucumbers: pickled, 125; cucumber salad dressing, 162

Currant jam, 172–73

Daikon tea (dried radish), 180, 214

Dairy products, 55; and yin and yang, 187

Dandelion, 103; dandelion coffee, 179

Dashi kombu seaweed, 120

Desserts, 94, 165–74; dessert pie dough, 94; acorn squash compote, 165–66; aduki brownies, 166; aduki muffins, 166; buckwheat muffins, 167; tangy applesauce, 167; apple-cranberry sauce, 167; chestnut cream pudding (blancmange), 168; quick couscous pudding, 168; gingerbread, 168–69; Indian corn pudding, 169; millet cake, 169–70; flourless oatmeal cookies, 170; Christmas rice pudding, 170–71; pies, 171; apple or fruit crisp, 171–72; squash pie, 172; currant jam, 172–73; fruit sherbet, 173; fresh fruit gelatin, 173; toppings for pies, cakes, and cookies, 174

Dulse, 118, 119, 120, 123, 214

Dyed teas, 54

Egg foo young, 153

Eggplant, 96

Eggs, 55–56

Fat: and protein content of sampling of common food (*chart*), 51; saturated fats, 55, 62*n*.; *see also* Oils

Fish, 36, 153–56; tiny dried (chirimen iriko), 36, 213; shellfish, 153; clam sauce with spaghetti, 154; fish chowder, 154–55; shrimp creole, 155; sole wrapped in a blanket, 155–56; classified according to yin and yang, 187; bonita flakes, 213

Flakes of grain, 60, 81–82; boiled flakes, 81; baked flakes, 81–82

Flour, 34, 60, 87; storing of, 37; *see also* Breads and other things made from flour

Food supplements, 45; vitamin pills, 46

Frozen food, 56

Fruits: fresh, 34; dried, 34; storing of, 38; tropical, 96; suggested for tempura, 112; fruit sherbet, 173; fresh fruit gelatin, 173; classified according to yin and yang, 187–88

Garlic, 104, 105

Gingerbread, 168–69

Goat's milk, 55

Gomasio (sesame salt), 29–30, 214

Grains, 23, 26, 33, 34, 60–85, 87, 95; rice, 23, 33, 61–68;

Grains—(*Continued*)
eating of whole grains, 26, 60, 77; buckwheat, 34, 70–72, 213; millet, 34, 75–77; oats, 34, 53, 74–75; storing of, 37; storing of cooked grains, 38; corn, 58, 72–74; importance of, in macrobiotic diet, 60–61, 95; cracked cereals, 60, 80; flakes of grain, 60, 81–82; milling of, into flour, 60, 87; barley, 68–70; wheat, 77–79; cream cereals, 80; grain milk (or kohkoh, or infant cereal, or koko), 82; sprouts made from grain, 82–83; noodles, 83–85; organically grown, 87; deep-fried grain croquettes, 113; grain coffee, 177–78; grain tea, 178; classified according to yin and yang, 187; *see also* specific name of grain

Greek spinach pie, 152

Hacho miso, 33
Hiziki seaweed, 33, 118, 119, 120, 123, 214
Honey, 53, 58, 59

Infant cereal, 82*n*.

Japanese salad press, 114

Kanten, *see* Agar-agar
Kasha, 34, 70–72, 214; kasha croquettes, 71–72; kasha spoon bread, 72
Kelp, 118
Knishes, 147–48; vegetable knishes, 147–49
Kohkoh, 82, 214

Koko, 82*n*.
Kombu seaweed, 119, 120–21, 123, 214; sautéed kombu, 121; basic kombu soup stock, 127
Kome miso, 33, 142
Kukicha tea, *see* Bancha tea
Kushi, Michio, 19
Kuzu, 156, 214

Leavening agents in bread doughs, 56
Leeks, 104, 105; sautéed, 106
Leftovers, storing of, 38
Legumes, *see* Beans
Lentils, 33; red lentils and rice, 140; curried lentils, 140; Mediterranean style lentils, 140
Lettuce, 104
Lima soy sauce, 34*n*., 214*n*.
Lotus root tea, 178–79

Macrobiotic source books, lists of, 210–11; cookbooks, 210; guidebooks by George Ohsawa, 210; other publications, 211
Macrobiotics: what macrobiotics is, 20; meaning of, 21; yin and yang, 22–25, 181–82; and vegetarianism, 23–24, 56; and cooking of foods, 27–31; foods excluded from diet, 54–59; travel, and eating macrobiotically, 189–90
Macrobiotics, list of commercial sources where material is available: stores and restaurants in U.S., 191–203; stores, restaurants, and centers outside U.S., 204–7;

220 INDEX

wholesale distributors in U.S., 208–9
Maple syrup, 53, 59
Marine algae, *see* Seaweed
Meat, and macrobiotic diet, 23, 24, 49, 56; processed meats, 56; *see also* Animal foods
Menus, suggested, 182–86; winter, 182–84; summer, 184–86
Mexican chili, 150–51
Millet, 34, 75–77; millet and onions, 76; millet casserole, 76; millet croquettes, 76–77; whole wheat bread with millet, 90; millet cake, 169–70
Minerals, 23, 26, 46, 49; found in food we eat (*chart*), 50
Mint tea, 177
Miso, 29, 33, 142–46, 214; miso paste, 33; tofu, 36, 145–46, 214; storing of, 37–38; miso pickles, 124–25; miso soup, 128; miso-wakame soup, 129; cream of miso soup, 135; what makes miso so beneficial, 141–45; miso "aging" process, 142–43; barley miso, 143; miso-vegetable stew, 143; miso-rice, 144; miso stew with vegetables, 144; miso-vegetable spoon bread, 144–45; miso béchamel sauce, 159; miso gravy, 159; simple miso spreads, 161; miso-vegetable spread, 161; miso-watercress spread, 161
Mochi, 67–68; aduki mochi, 67–68
Molasses, 53, 58
Mu tea, 35, 179, 214
Muffins: corn, 91; aduki, 166; buckwheat, 167
Mugi miso, 33
Mugicha, *see* Barley tea

Nato kombu seaweed, 120–21
Noodles, 35, 83–85; udon, 83, 214; soba, 83, 214; homemade buckwheat noodles, 84; French dumpling strips, 84–85; salad with noodles and corn, 116–17
Nori seaweed, 33–34, 119, 123, 214
Nuts, 34, 46; storing of, 38

Oats, 34, 53, 74–75; rolled, 34; oatmeal, 74; old-fashioned oat porridge, 75; oat flakes crust, 93; flourless oatmeal cookies, 170
Ohsawa, George, books on macrobiotics by, 19, 210
Oils: for macrobiotic cooking, 34; vegetable oils, 44, 53, 57; and fats, 53; refined oil margarine, and hydrogenated oils, 56–58; "cold pressed," 57; olive oil, imported (virgin), 57; varieties of, 57
Onion family, 76, 96, 97, 104–6; millet and onions, 76; cutting of onions, 96, 97; sautéed leeks, 106; creamed parsnips and onions, 106; wakame and onions, 121; aduki beans and onions, 138; onion sauce béchamel, 159; onion butter, 161–62

Pancakes: corn, 73–74; pancakes, crepes, and waffles, 92–93; whole wheat, 92; tempura batter used in, 113
Parsnips, 106; creamed, with onions, 106
Peanut butter, 35
Pickles, 124–25; storing of, 124; simple Chinese cabbage pickles, 124; miso pickles,

INDEX 221

Pickles—(*Continued*)
124–25; pickled cucumbers, 125

Pies, 171; toppings for, 174; *see also* Crusts and pie dough

Piroski, 148, 149

Pizza: macrobiotic style, 149–50; aduki or chickpea pizza, 150; pizza rolls, 150

Popcorn, organic, 36

Potatoes, 96

Processed foods, 55

Protein, 49; from animal products, 49; protein and fat content of sampling of common foods (*chart*), 51

Publications on macrobiotics, lists of, 210–11

Radish, dried, *see* Daikon tea

Refrigeration of food, 37

Rice, 23, 33, 61–68; brown rice, 23, 33, 61–68, 213; storing of cooked rice, 38; as nutritionally superior grain, 61; yin and yang, 62; boiled rice, basic preparation, 62–63; pressure-cooked rice, 63; baked rice, 64; rice or wholegrain porridge, 64; rice cream made from prepared powder, 64; fried rice, 65; fried rice with vegetables, 65; sushi, 65–66; sweet brown rice, 67; aduki mochi, 67–68; wheat berries and rice, 77–78; rice kayu, 89; whole rice bread, 89; whole rice crust, 94; rice balls and seaweed wrappings, 121–22; red lentils and rice, 140; miso-rice, 144; Christmas rice pudding, 170–71

Rye and barley coffee, 178

Salad dressings, 162–63; cucumber dressing, 162; umeboshi dressing, 162; green goddess dressing, 162–63

Salads, 114–17; pressed salad, 114–15; summer salad, 115; beet and watercress salad, 115–16; Greek salad, 116; salad with noodles and corn, 116–17; quick boiled salad, 117

Salt, use of, in cooking, 28–30, 98; unrefined white sea salt, 28, 35, 214; sources of salt, other than sea water, 29; sesame salt, or gomasio, 29–30, 214; major ways in which salt can affect our bodies, 29

Salted plums (umeboshi), 29, 35, 38, 214; burdock and salted plums, 100; pits of, 114*n*.; umeboshi salad dressing, 162; umeboshi juice, 176, 179–80

Sauces, 99, 157–63; béchamel, 99, 102, 158–59; clear sauce, 159–60; simple tahini and tamari sauces, 160

Sautéing of vegetables, 97–98; green vegetables, 100–101, 103; dandelion greens, 103; lettuce, 104; leeks, 106; kombu, 121

Scallions, 104, 105

Sea salt, 28, 35, 214

Sea vegetables, 102, 118–23; carrots and sea vegetables, 102; varieties of, 118; *see also* Seaweed

Seawater, 23, 28, 29

Seaweed, 33–34, 38, 118; as rich source of minerals, 46, 49; varieties of, 118; seaweed wrappings for rice balls, 121–22; food content and mineral content of varieties of (*chart*), 123

Seeds, 34; storing of, 38; sesame seeds, 38, 46; pits of salted plums, 114n.; beans, 136–41

Sesame: sesame salt (gomasio), 29–30, 214; sesame seeds, 38, 46; sesame glaze, 174; sesame butter, 214

Shallots, 78n., 104–5

Soba noodles, 83, 214

Soft drinks and diet colas, 58

Soups, 38, 126–35; storing of, 38; clear stock and broths, 127–28; basic kombu stock, 127; simple egg drop soup, 128; miso soup, 128; miso-wakame soup, 129; barley-split pea soup, 129–30; old-fashioned vegetable soup, 130; country vegetable soup, 130–31; fresh corn chowder, 131; minestrone, 131–32; thick turnip soup, 132; cream soups, 132–35; cream of celery, 133; squash potage, 133–34; cream of cauliflower soup, 134–35; cream of miso soup, 135; fish chowder, 154–55

Soy sauce, tamari, 34–35, 214

Soybean miso, see Miso

Spices, 36, 58

Spinach: in cream sauce, 107; Greek spinach pie, 152

Spreads: simple miso spreads, 161; miso-vegetable spread, 161; miso-watercress spread, 161; onion butter, 161–62; bean spread, 163; aduki spread, 163

Spring water, 59, 86

Sprouts: made from grain, 82–83; made from beans, 83

Squash: baked, 108; squash potage, 133–34; acorn squash compote, 165–66; squash pie, 172

Stocking kitchen for macrobiotic cooking, 32–36

Storing of food, 37–39

Succotash—American Indian misickquatash, 107

Sugar, 23, 53, 58–59

Sushi, 65–66

Sweetening agents, 58–59; see also specific name of sweetening agent

Tahini sauce, 160

Tamari, 29, 34–35, 37, 38, 160, 214

Tap water, 59, 86; treating of, 59, 87

Teas: bancha tea, 33, 177, 213; mu tea, 35, 179, 214; dyed, 54; mint tea, 177; grain tea, 178; lotus root tea, 178–79; burdock tea, 179; daikon tea (dried radish), 180, 214; barley tea (mugicha), 214

Tempura, 102, 109–13, 214; tempura batters, 108, 110, 112; vegetables or fruits suggested for, 112; tempura dip, 160

Tofu, 36, 145–46, 214; homemade tofu, 145–46; served with chop suey, 152

Tomatoes, 96

Torro kombu seaweed, 120, 121

Travel, and eating macrobiotically, 189–90; stores and restaurants in U.S., list of, 191–203; stores, restaurants, and centers outside U.S., list of, 204–7; wholesale distributors in U.S., list of, 208–9

Tropical vegetables and fruits, 96

Turnips: baked, 108; thick turnip soup, 132

Udon noodles, 83, 214
Umeboshi, see Salted plums
Utensils as basic tools, 40–44; pressure cooker, 40, 42, 43; materials preferred for cookware and serving items, 40; use of wooden implements in handling food during cooking, 40, 42; basic items recommended, 41–42; miscellaneous items, 42–43; use of detergents or cleansers on, 44; removing burned food stuck to, 44; preventing rust of, 44

Vegetable oils, 44, 53, 57
see also Oils
Vegetables: fresh, 34; organically grown, 34; storing of fresh and of root, 38; storing of sautéed, 38; wilted, 38; fried rice with vegetables, 65; barley with vegetables, 69; as secondary foods in macrobiotic diet, 95–96; potatoes, tomatoes, eggplant, and macrobiotic diet, 96; tropical, 96; idea of yin and yang applied in preparation of, 96; washing and scrubbing of fresh, 96; cutting of, 96, 97; onion family, 96, 97, 104–5; carrots, 96, 97, 101–2; preparing several together, 96–97; sautéing of, 97–98; use of salt in cooking of, 98; various methods of cooking, 98; broccoli, 98–99; Brussels sprouts, 99; burdock, 99–100, 213; sautéed green vegetables, 100–101, 103; sea vegetables, 102, 118–23; cauliflower, 102–3; cabbage, 103, 124; dandelion, 103, 179; lettuce, 104; parsnips, 106; spinach, 107, 152; squash, 108, 133–34, 165–66, 172; turnips, 108, 132; suggested for tempura, 112; vegetable dumplings, 113; cucumbers, 125, 162; old-fashioned vegetable soup, 130; country vegetable soup, 130–31; miso stew with vegetables, 143, 144; miso-vegetable spoon bread, 144–45; vegetable knishes, 147–49; vegetable aspic, 173; classified according to yin and yang, 187; see also specific name of vegetable
Vegetarianism: and macrobiotics, 23–24, 56; switch from, to macrobiotics, 32
Vitamins, 26, 46; vitamin pills, 46; found in foods we eat (chart), 47; vitamin loss in cooking (chart), 48

Waffles, 93
Wakame, 118, 119, 121, 123, 214; wakame and onion, 121; miso-wakame soup, 129
Water: seawater, 23, 28, 29; spring, 59, 86; tap, 59, 86–87; treating of tap water, 59, 87; in making of bread, 86–87
Watercress: carrots and watercress, 101–2; beet and watercress salad, 115–16; miso-watercress spread, 161
Wheat, 77–79; whole cooked wheat, 77; wheat berries and rice, 77–78; wheat berries and black beans, 78, 139; fried wheat berries, 78; wheat products, 79; whole wheat bread with millet, 90; whole wheat pancakes, 92

224 INDEX

Wheat products, 79; bulgar, 79, 213; couscous, 79, 214; cracked wheat, 79, 80; wheat flakes, 79

Whole foods, eating of, 26; grains, 26, 60, 77

Wooden instruments: use of, in handling food during cooking, 40; wooden spoons, 42, 43, 44; drying of, 44

Yin and yang, 22–25; and macrobiotics, 22–25; understanding of terms as applied to daily cooking, 22–24; listing of foods classified according to, 25, 187–88; factors in food preparation, 27–31; time and pressure as yang factors in food preparation, 30; preference for cookware made out of yang materials, 40; application of, in preparation of vegetables, 96